DAY HIKES IN
Yosemite
NATIONAL PARK

80 GREAT HIKES

Robert Stone
3rd EDITION

Day Hike Books, Inc.

RED LODGE, MONTANA

Published by Day Hike Books, Inc.
P.O. Box 865
Red Lodge, Montana 59068
www.dayhikebooks.com

Distributed by The Globe Pequot Press
246 Goose Lane
P.O. Box 480
Guilford, CT 06437-0480
800-243-0495 (direct order) · 800-820-2329 (fax order)
www.globe-pequot.com

Photographs by Robert Stone
Design by Paula Doherty

The author has made every attempt to provide accurate information in this book. However, trail routes and features may change—please use common sense and forethought, and be mindful of your own capabilities. Let this book guide you, but be aware that each hiker assumes responsibility for their own safety. The author and publisher do not assume any responsibility for loss, damage, or injury caused through the use of this book.

Cover photo: Taft Point, Hike 59

Back cover photo: Unicorn Creek
en route to Elizabeth Lake, Hike 16

ALSO BY ROBERT STONE

Day Hikes On the California Central Coast

Day Hikes On the California Southern Coast

Day Hikes Around Sonoma County

Day Hikes Around Napa Valley

Day Hikes Around Big Sur

Day Hikes Around Monterey and Carmel

Day Hikes In San Luis Obispo County, California

Day Hikes Around Santa Barbara

Day Hikes Around Ventura County

Day Hikes Around Los Angeles

Day Hikes Around Orange County

Day Hikes In Sedona, Arizona

Day Hikes In Sequoia & Kings Canyon Nat'l. Parks

Day Hikes In Yellowstone National Park

Day Hikes In Grand Teton National Park

Day Hikes In the Beartooth Mountains

Day Hikes Around Bozeman, Montana

Day Hikes Around Missoula, Montana

Day Hikes On Oahu

Day Hikes On Maui

Day Hikes On Kauai

Day Hikes In Hawaii

Table of Contents

THE HIKES

Highway 120
Lee Vining to East Park Entrance

Tioga Road

Hetch Hetchy to Tioga Road

Yosemite Valley
Merced River Gorge to Tenaya Canyon

Glacier Point Road

Wawona Area

South of Yosemite
South Park Entrance to Oakhurst

Hiking Yosemite

Yosemite is one of the world's most loved national parks. It is best known for Yosemite Valley, with its huge granite monoliths and long waterfalls; the rolling, boulder-strewn meadows along the Tuolumne River; and the rugged, snow-capped peaks of the Sierras.

The park lies in central California on the western slope of the Sierra Nevada Range. The dramatic topography was sculpted by glaciers 10,000 years ago. The elevation ranges from 2,000 feet to 13,000 feet along the eastern boundary. Even though the park has 196 miles of roads, more than 90 percent of Yosemite is roadless wilderness and home to more than 750 miles of trails.

This collection of 80 day hikes in and around Yosemite provides access to all of the well-known park features as well as many lesser-known trails and destinations. Highlights include incredible waterfalls, granite monoliths, expansive alpine meadows, and unforgettable views from unique perspectives that are only accessible from the hiking trails. Outstanding scenery surrounds every trail regardless of its difficulty.

The crown jewel of the park is Yosemite Valley, a picturesque, seven-mile gorge lined with 3,000-foot granite massifs, smooth domes, and an abundance of spectacular waterfalls that drop over the cliffs to the Merced River at the valley floor. Half Dome, Clouds Rest, Cathedral Rock, Three Arches, and the largest granite rock on earth—El Capitan—rise dramatically out of the valley. Yosemite Falls plunges over 2,400 feet at the end of the valley, the longest falls in North America and fifth longest in the world. Hikes 40—53 explore the magnificent valley. Hikes range from easy paths along the Merced River to heart-pounding climbs up the granite cliffs.

To the north of the valley is scenic Tuolumne Meadows, formed by an enormous glacier 60 miles long and 2,000 feet thick. Tuolumne Meadows is the largest subalpine meadow in the Sierra Nevada Range. It measures 2.5 miles long by a half mile wide and sits at an elevation of 8,600 feet. The glacier also formed polished granite domes, alpine lakes, and deep canyons. The Tuolumne River carves a winding path through the terrain.

Tioga Road accesses the Tuolumne region. The road is the highest paved auto route in California. The road (Highway 120) enters the park at the Tioga Pass entrance at 9,945 feet (Hikes 1–6), then crosses the entire north-central section of the park. Hikes 7–31 lie along the road and offer access to the mid- to upper regions of the park, characterized by rugged alpine peaks and cobalt blue lakes (back cover photo). Several of these hikes offer distinct opportunities to see Yosemite Valley from its "back" side. (Tioga Road is closed November–May.)

The Tuolumne River drains through the alpine meadow to the Hetch Hetchy Reservoir in a remote, beautiful valley on the west side of Yosemite. Hikes 32–36 are located near the reservoir and along the high, narrow river gorge below the dam.

Three giant sequoia groves are located within the park— Mariposa Grove, Merced Grove, and Tuolumne Grove. Hikes 37–39 explore the Merced and Tuolumne Groves. These small but impressive groves of towering trees fit the scale of the park's awe-inspiring geological features. A fourth group of giant sequoias—Nelder Grove—is located south of the park (Hikes 75–77).

South of Yosemite Valley is Glacier Point Road, Hikes 54–66. The road leads along the valley's towering south rim. Highlights include vistas from atop 3,000-foot cliffs (cover photo) and spectacular panoramas of the valley. Several trails travel across the top of the rim as well as offer routes back down to Yosemite

Valley along unforgettable cliffside paths. The road also provides access to several quiet forest strolls, a welcome respite from the crowds. (Glacier Point Road is closed November—May.)

Near the south entrance of the park is the Wawona basin and meadow, home to the historic Wawona Hotel. Hikes 67—70 are forested hikes along the South Fork Merced River and its tributaries. Hikes 71—72 are located in Mariposa Grove, the park's most visited grove, with an impressive display of over 300 giant sequoias.

Heading southward from the park leads through deep forests that offer solitude and quiet reflection—Hikes 73—80. Creekside trails lead to cascading waterfalls. A group of giant sequoias preserved in the Nelder Grove includes several outstanding examples of these majestic trees.

To choose a hike that is appropriate to your ability, time, and interests, glance through the hikes' summaries and statistics. An overall map on page 12 identifies the general locations of the hikes and major roads. Several other regional maps (underlined in the table of contents), as well as the maps for each hike, illustrate the access roads and trail routes. To hike farther into the backcountry, relevant maps are listed under the statistics.

A few basic necessities will make your hike more pleasurable. Wear supportive, comfortable hiking shoes and layered clothing. Take along hats, sunscreen, sunglasses, drinking water, snacks, and appropriate outerwear. The weather often changes quickly at these high elevations. Use good judgement about your capabilities—reference the hiking statistics and summaries for an approximation of difficulty, allowing extra time for exploration.

These hikes include some of the best scenery in Yosemite. Your time on the trails will undoubtedly add to your appreciation of this incredible park. Enjoy your hike!

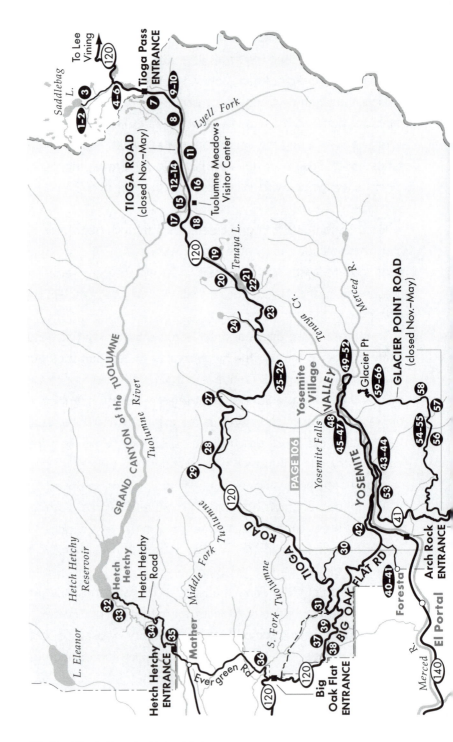

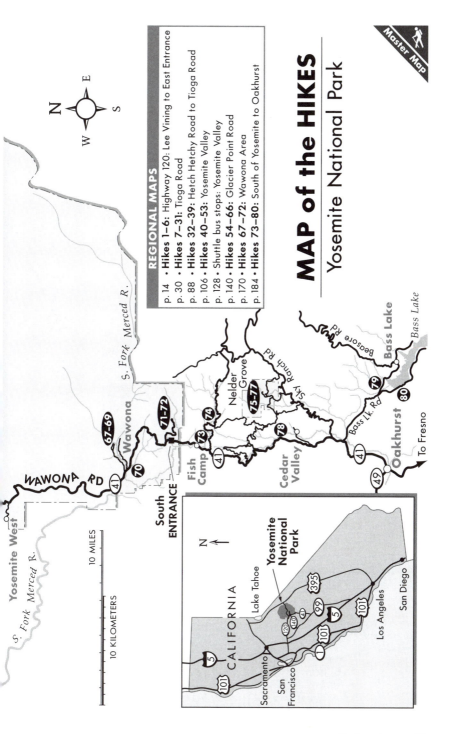

MAP of the HIKES
Yosemite National Park

REGIONAL MAPS

p. 14 • **Hikes 1–6**: Highway 120: Lee Vining to East Entrance
p. 30 • **Hikes 7–31**: Tioga Road
p. 88 • **Hikes 32–39**: Hetch Hetchy Road to Tioga Road
p. 106 • **Hikes 40–53**: Yosemite Valley
p. 128 • Shuttle bus stops: Yosemite Valley
p. 140 • **Hikes 54–66**: Glacier Point Road
p. 170 • **Hikes 67–72**: Wawona Area
p. 184 • **Hikes 73–80**: South of Yosemite to Oakhurst

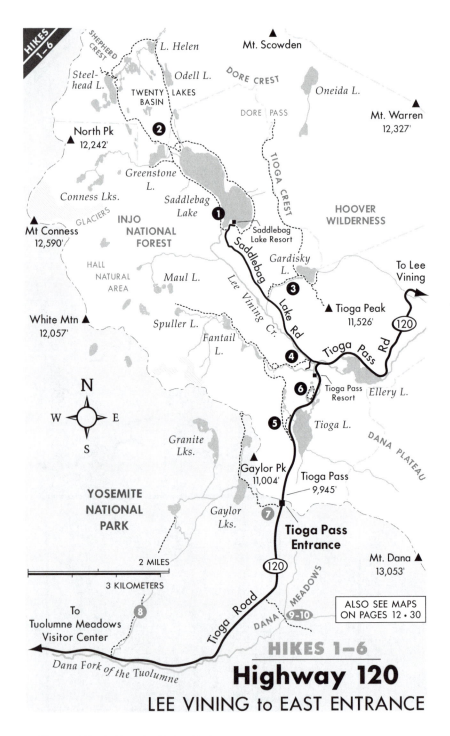

SHEPHERD CREST

L. Helen

Mt. Scowden ▲

Steel-
head L.

Odell L.

DORE CREST

Oneida L.

TWENTY LAKES
BASIN

DORE PASS

Mt. Warren ▲
12,327'

North Pk
▲ 12,242'

TIOGA CREST

Greenstone
L.

Conness Lks.

Saddlebag
Lake

HOOVER
WILDERNESS

GLACIERS

INJO
NATIONAL
FOREST

❶

Saddlebag
Lake Resort

Mt Conness ▲
12,590'

Gardisky
L.

To Lee
Vining

HALL
NATURAL
AREA

Maul L.

Lee Vining Cr.

Saddlebag Lake Rd

❸

❷

▲ Tioga Peak
11,526'

120

White Mtn ▲
12,057'

Spuller L.

Fantail
L.

❹

Tioga Pass Rd

❻

Tioga Pass
Resort

Ellery L.

N

W ✦ **E**

S

❺

Tioga L.

DANA PLATEAU

Granite
Lks.

Gaylor Pk ▲
11,004'

Tioga Pass
9,945'

YOSEMITE
NATIONAL
PARK

Gaylor
Lks.

❼

**Tioga Pass
Entrance**

Mt. Dana ▲
13,053'

2 MILES

3 KILOMETERS

120

ALSO SEE MAPS
ON PAGES 12 • 30

To
Tuolumne Meadows
Visitor Center

⑧

Tioga Road

DANA MEADOWS

⑨-⑩

HIKES 1-6

Dana Fork of the Tuolumne

Highway 120
LEE VINING to EAST ENTRANCE

1. Saddlebag Lake

Hiking distance: 3.5-mile loop
Hiking time: 2 hours
Elevation gain: 100 feet
Maps: U.S.G.S. Tioga Pass

map
page 17

Summary of hike: Saddlebag Lake is a huge 10,000-foot-high lake three miles outside of Yosemite in the eastern High Sierras. The 340-acre lake lies within the Inyo National Forest and is adjacent to the rugged Hoover Wilderness, tucked beneath Tioga Crest and surrounded by 12,000-foot mountains. At the trailhead is a cafe, general store, and boat rental. This popular fishing area is teeming with a variety of trout. A convenient water taxi is available to quickly arrive at the far north end of the 1.5-mile-long lake. This hike circles Saddlebag Lake past Greenstone Lake, with awesome vistas of Tioga Crest, North Peak, Mount Conness, and Shepherd Crest. The water taxi offers a shorter option for exploring the Twenty Lakes Basin and the Hoover Wilderness (Hike 2).

Driving directions: From the Tioga Pass park entrance, drive 2.2 miles east on Highway 120/Tioga Pass Road to Saddlebag Lake Road. Turn left and drive 2.4 miles to the day-use parking lot at the end of the road (above the boat launch). The last 0.8 miles is unpaved. An additional overnight parking lot is on the right, just before reaching the end of the road.

From Lee Vining at Highway 395, drive 10 miles west on Highway 120/Tioga Pass Road to Saddlebag Lake Road. Turn right and follow the directions above.

Hiking directions: Walk back down the road below the dam. Take the dirt road on the right, and descend to the base of the dam. Cross the headwaters of Lee Vining Creek, pass a metal gate, and climb up to the footpath on the west end of the dam. Take the posted trail north along the foot of the steep 11,239-foot mountain. The rocky, undulating path meanders along the mountainside 50—80 feet above scenic Saddlebag Lake. At a half mile curve left, with vistas into the Hoover Wilderness,

Shepherd Crest, and North Peak. At 1.2 miles, leave the rocky mountain slope, and descend into the alpine tundra, overlooking Greenstone Lake. Head toward the lake and cross a log bridge over the stream connecting Greenstone Lake with Saddlebag Lake. Bear right and follow the main trail 100 yards to a posted junction. The left fork leads into Twenty Lakes Basin (Hike 2). For this hike, bear right, passing two connector paths to the water taxi dock. The second path is across from the return route of the Twenty Lakes Basin loop. Pass a ranger cabin on the north shore of Saddlebag Lake, and curve south on the forested path. The trail, tucked between Saddlebag Lake and Tioga Crest, was the old tungsten mining road, abandoned in the 1950s. Pass the peninsula jutting into the lake, creating the saddlebag shape. The conifer forest ends and the path continues along the exposed, barren slope above the lake, crossing two stream drainages. At the south end of the lake, curve right, emerging at the east end of the parking lot.

2. Twenty Lakes Basin Loop

Hiking distance: 5-mile loop with water taxi across
Saddlebag Lake
8.5-mile loop hiking around Saddlebag Lake
Hiking time: 3—5 hours
Elevation gain: 300 feet
Maps: U.S.G.S. Tioga Pass and Dunderberg Peak

map
page 19

Summary of hike: The Twenty Lakes Basin lies northeast of Yosemite National Park just below the eastern escarpment of the Sierras. The basin is between Shepherd Crest and Tioga Crest in the 47,916-acre Hoover Wilderness. Glacier-scoured ridges and majestic peaks surround the expansive alpine landscape. The trail begins above 10,000 feet on the north end of Saddlebag Lake. The scenic route passes numerous ponds and eight additional lakes, including Greenstone Lake, Wasco Lake, Steelhead Lake, Excelsior Lake, Shamrock Lake, Lake Helen, Odell Lake, and Hummingbird Lake. Each lake has its own unique character.

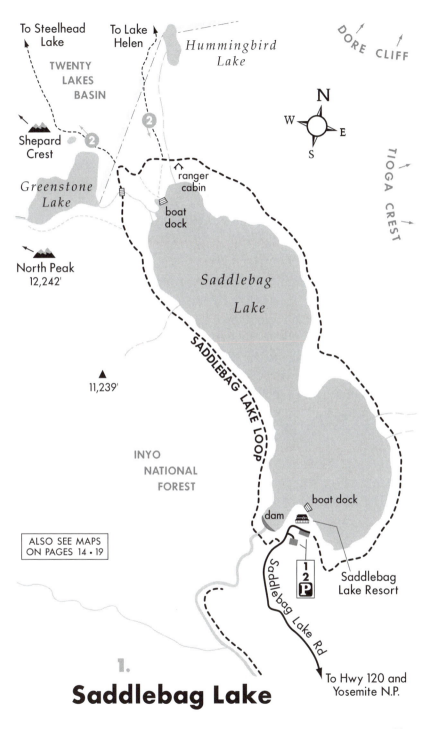

To Steelhead Lake

To Lake Helen

Hummingbird Lake

DORE CLIFF

TWENTY LAKES BASIN

N
W E
S

TIOGA CREST

Shepard Crest

Greenstone Lake

ranger cabin

boat dock

North Peak
12,242'

Saddlebag Lake

11,239'

SADDLEBAG LAKE LOOP

INYO NATIONAL FOREST

boat dock

dam

ALSO SEE MAPS ON PAGES 14 • 19

1 2 P

Saddlebag Lake Resort

Saddlebag Lake Rd

1.

Saddlebag Lake

To Hwy 120 and Yosemite N.P.

Steelhead Lake sits in a glacially carved rock bowl. Shamrock Lake has numerous fingers of land extending into the lake with picturesque, pine-dotted islands. Helen Lake sits in the bottom of a deep depression, completely surrounded by mountains.

Driving directions: From the Tioga Pass park entrance, drive 2.2 miles east on Highway 120/Tioga Pass Road to Saddlebag Lake Road. Turn left and drive 2.4 miles to the day-use parking lot at the end of the road (above the boat launch). The last 0.8 miles is unpaved. An additional overnight parking lot is on the right, just before reaching the end of the road.

From Lee Vining at Highway 395, drive 10 miles west on Highway 120/Tioga Pass Road to Saddlebag Lake Road. Turn right and follow the directions above.

Hiking directions: If hiking around Saddlebag Lake, follow the hiking directions for Hike 1 to the posted junction with the Twenty Lakes Basin Loop, then bear left. If taking the water taxi, from the dock on the north end of Saddlebag Lake, head up the hill to a T-junction with the Saddlebag Lake Loop Trail. Bear left to the posted Hoover Wilderness boundary.

Sign the register and enter the wilderness. Stay to the right, skirting the east edge of Greenstone Lake. Ascend the slope, passing a pond on the left to an overlook of the pond, Greenstone Lake, Saddlebag Lake, and Tioga Crest. The prominent peaks of Shepherd Crest, Mount Conness, Conness Glacier, and North Peak loom in the west. The granite peaks lie on the boundary between Yosemite National Park and the Hoover Wilderness. Follow the rock-marked path above Wasco Lake on the left beneath North Peak, rising 2,000 feet above the trail. At the north end of Wasco Lake, follow the stream directly toward jagged Excelsior Mountain to Steelhead Lake. Stroll along the east side of the lake on an elevated shelf, overlooking the waterfall cascading off the granite rock wall into the lake. At the north end of the lake, curve right, passing gorgeous ponds and Excelsior Lake to a signed fork. The old road continues west to the abandoned Hess Tungsten Mine above Steelhead Lake. Bear right and cross Mill Creek, the outlet stream, on a log bridge to a

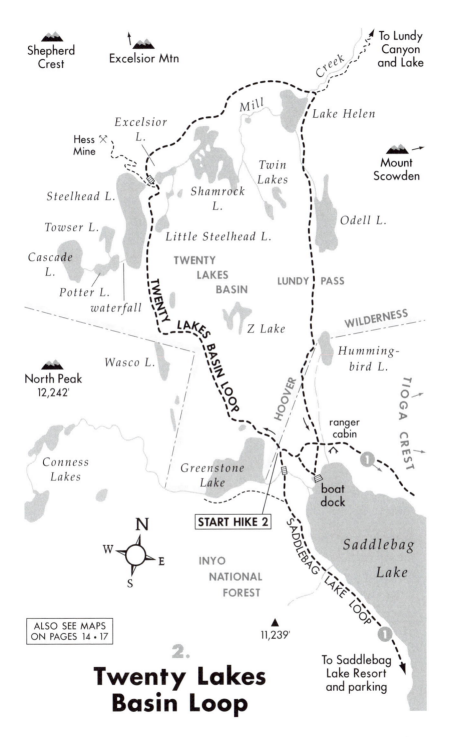

Shepherd Crest

Excelsior Mtn

To Lundy Canyon and Lake

Mill Creek

Excelsior L.

Hess Mine

Steelhead L.

Towser L.

Cascade L.

Potter L. waterfall

Shamrock L.

Little Steelhead L.

TWENTY LAKES BASIN

Lake Helen

Twin Lakes

Mount Scowden

Odell L.

LUNDY PASS

WILDERNESS

Z Lake

North Peak 12,242'

Wasco L.

Hummingbird L.

TIOGA CREST

HOOVER

TWENTY LAKES BASIN LOOP

Conness Lakes

Greenstone Lake

ranger cabin

1

boat dock

START HIKE 2

N
W   E
S

INYO NATIONAL FOREST

Saddlebag Lake

SADDLEBAG LAKE LOOP

1

ALSO SEE MAPS ON PAGES 14 • 17

11,239'

To Saddlebag Lake Resort and parking

2.
Twenty Lakes Basin Loop

footpath. Climb the rocky hillside and descend to multi-armed Shamrock Lake, a clover-shaped lake with several peninsulas and rock islands. Pass the 50-foot rocky cascade feeding Shamrock Lake and cross a talus slope. Follow cairns to an overlook of Helen Lake and Mount Scowden. Descend the rocky cliff to the northwest corner of Helen Lake. Walk over more talus along the north end of Helen Lake to the head of Lundy Canyon. Cross Mill Creek to a posted junction. The left fork follows Mill Creek down Lundy Canyon to Lundy Lake. Bear right along the east side of Lake Helen. Climb the slope out of the deep lake basin. Atop the short, steep climb is Odell Lake. Traverse the cliffs along the west side of Odell Lake, and stroll through the exposed, rolling terrain over 10,320-foot Lundy Pass. Skirt the west side of Hummingbird Lake, sitting in a bowl at the base of Tioga Crest. Leave the Hoover Wilderness and descend to the north shore of Saddlebag Lake. Cross the Saddlebag Lake Loop Trail to the water taxi dock.

To hike back on the east side of the lake, bear left and continue with the hiking directions for Hike 1.

3. Gardisky Lake

Hiking distance: 2.6 miles round trip
Hiking time: 1.5 hours
Elevation gain: 760 feet
Maps: U.S.G.S. Tioga Pass and Mount Dana

Summary of hike: Gardisky Lake is tucked beneath Tioga Crest just outside of the Hoover Wilderness in the Inyo National Forest. It was named in honor of Russian immigrant Al Gardisky, a Tioga Pass innkeeper in the early 1900s who named 15 lakes in the protected 3,883-acre Hall Natural Area. Gardisky Lake is nestled at 10,483 feet in a large, sloping meadow basin on the left flank of Tioga Peak above Saddlebag Lake. On the west edge of the alpine lake are clear, shallow ponds. The short but steep hike to Gardisky Lake climbs the east wall of the Lee Vining Creek

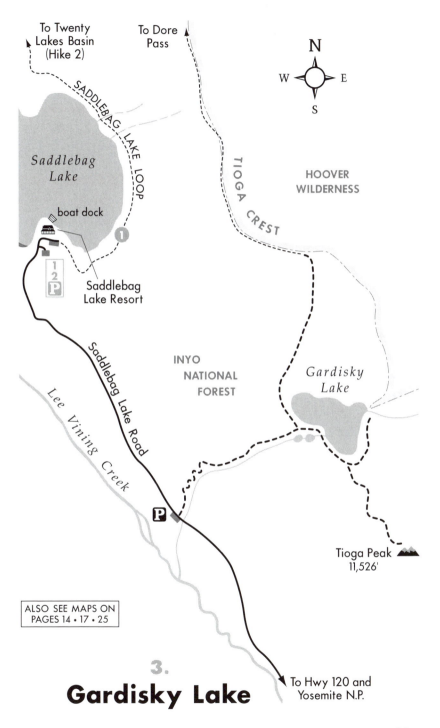

To Twenty Lakes Basin (Hike 2)

To Dore Pass

N
W ● E
S

SADDLEBAG LAKE LOOP

Saddlebag Lake

TIOGA CREST

HOOVER WILDERNESS

boat dock

Saddlebag Lake Resort

1 2 P

INYO NATIONAL FOREST

Gardisky Lake

Saddlebag Lake Road

Lee Vining Creek

P

Tioga Peak 11,526'

ALSO SEE MAPS ON PAGES 14 • 17 • 25

3.
Gardisky Lake

To Hwy 120 and Yosemite N.P.

drainage. The trail follows a tributary of Lee Vining Creek through a metamorphic terrain with lodgepole pines and twisted whitebark pines. Throughout the hike are spectacular vistas of the Eastern High Sierras.

Driving directions: From the Tioga Pass park entrance, drive 2.2 miles east on Highway 120/Tioga Pass Road to Saddlebag Lake Road. Turn left and drive 1.1 miles to the posted trailhead parking lot on the left.

From Lee Vining at Highway 395, drive 10 miles west on Highway 120/Tioga Pass Road to Saddlebag Lake Road. Turn right and drive 1.1 miles to the posted trailhead parking lot on the left.

Hiking directions: Cross Saddlebag Lake Road to the posted trailhead. Head uphill into the pine forest. Steadily zigzag up the mountain, gaining 600 feet in the first 0.6 miles. Emerge from the forest to sweeping vistas down the Lee Vining Creek drainage. Continue climbing, following the north edge of the willow-lined stream. The grade eases as the trail reaches the lower end of the sloping meadow, framed by stunted whitebark pine. Cross the spongy alpine tundra in the broad meadow between Tioga Peak and the green sloping hills of Tioga Crest. The trail fades in the treeless landscape as you pass a couple of tarns on the right, reaching the west end of Gardisky Lake.

There are several options to extend the hike. To explore the lake, follow the south side of the lake to the right. With a bit of scrambling through the brush, head north to the lake's outlet stream overlooking Lee Vining Canyon and across the Mono Lake Basin. To ascend 11,513-foot Tioga Peak, head south (right) up the rocky slope, gaining a thousand feet in 0.6 miles. To traverse Tioga Crest, head north (left) toward the saddle. The Tioga Crest ridgetop is in a half mile. Follow the ridge 2 miles to Dore Pass, overlooking Saddlebag Lake and Oneida Lake.

4. Mine Creek to Fantail Lake and Spuller Lake

Hiking distance: 4 miles round trip
Hiking time: 2 hours
Elevation gain: 750 feet
Maps: U.S.G.S. Tioga Pass and Mount Dana

map
page 25

Summary of hike: White Mountain straddles the boundary between Yosemite National Park and the Hoover Wilderness. Mine Creek cascades down the east flank of White Mountain, forming a chain of crystal clear mountain lakes before joining Lee Vining Creek near the Tioga Pass Resort. The creek begins at Spuller Lake on a 10,273-foot shelf and tumbles down a small, scenic valley into island-dotted Fantail Lake, Mine Lake, and Shell Lake, backed by a string of glaciers and the majestic peaks of the Sierra Crest. The creek weaves around the abandoned silver mining community of Bennettville (built in the 1870s) before merging with Lee Vining Creek. This hike follows the creek upstream from Junction Campground by Tioga Pass Road to Spuller Lake.

Driving directions: From the Tioga Pass park entrance, drive 2.2 miles east on Highway 120/Tioga Pass Road to Saddlebag Lake Road. Turn left and drive 100 yards to the parking spaces on the left by the Bennettville Plaque, just before entering Junction Campground.

From Lee Vining at Highway 395, drive 10 miles west on Highway 120/Tioga Pass Road to Saddlebag Lake Road. Turn right and drive 100 yards to the parking spaces on the left by the Bennettville Plaque, just before entering the Junction Campground.

Hiking directions: Cross the bridge over Lee Vining Creek to the posted trailhead at the Junction Campground entrance. Bear right and follow Lee Vining Creek upstream along the southern base of Tioga Peak. Zigzag up the hillside and traverse the slope above the campground to the east edge of the shady Mine Creek drainage. Head up the rocky, rust-colored gorge, paralleling the cascading Mine Creek with small waterfalls and pools. Cross two tributary streams and a beautiful 10-foot cataract. At 0.9 miles, enter the site of Bennettville and the two historically restored structures (also see Hike 5). After exploring the townsite, continue along Mine Creek to the southeast tip of Shell Lake, backed by cliffs rising 1,200 feet from the lake's west shore. Follow the east edge of Shell Lake to its north tip, and pass Mine Lake with a small island. Enter the Hall Natural Area to Fantail Lake, bounded by a cirque of mountains along the south, east and north sides. Continue following the watercourse across alpine tundra, leaving Fantail Lake and passing a 20-foot waterfall. Climb 300 feet up the rocky, alpine draw to Spuller Lake. Cross the north side of the lake to an overlook on a hill. This is the turn-around spot.

To hike farther, it is an easy stroll north to Maul Lake and Green Treble Lake.

5. Bennettville
GREAT SIERRA WAGON ROAD

Hiking distance: 3.5 miles round trip
Hiking time: 2 hours
Elevation gain: 100 feet
Maps: U.S.G.S. Tioga Pass

map
page 27

Summary of hike: Bennettville is an old silver mining camp dating back to the 1870s. The camp is located on the edge of Mine Creek in the Inyo National Forest, between the east park boundary and Tioga Peak. The abandoned 19th century community originally had 14 buildings. Only two of the historic structures remain—the assay office and a two-story barn. The weathered buildings were restored in 1993. The hike begins less than a mile outside Yosemite National Park, across the road from Tioga Lake. The trail follows the historic Great Sierra Wagon Road, a dirt road built in 1883 by the Great Sierra Silver Mining Company. The road was used to bring supplies and equipment to the company headquarters in Bennettville and to the Tioga "Sheepherder" Mine. It was also used to transport silver ore out

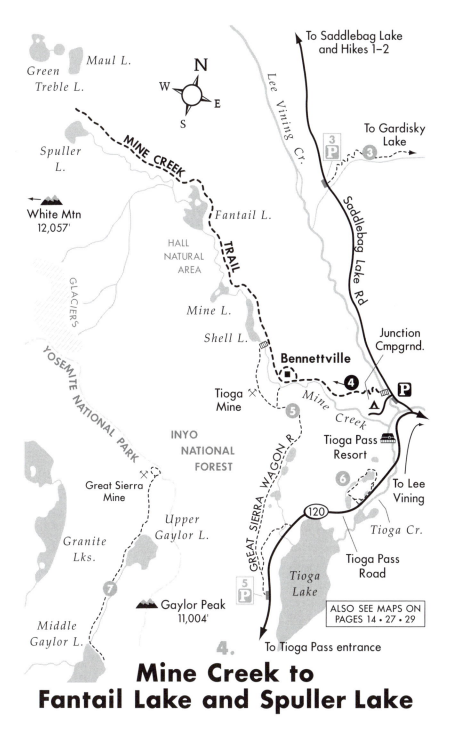

To Saddlebag Lake
and Hikes 1–2

Green
Treble L.

Maul L.

Spuller
L.

N
W ✦ **E**
S

MINE CREEK

Lee Vining Cr.

To Gardisky
Lake

White Mtn
12,057'

Fantail L.

HALL
NATURAL
AREA

TRAIL

Saddlebag Lake Rd

GLACIERS

Mine L.

Shell L.

Junction
Cmpgrnd.

YOSEMITE NATIONAL PARK

Bennettville

Mine Creek

Tioga
Mine

INYO
NATIONAL
FOREST

❺

❹

Tioga Pass
Resort

Great Sierra
Mine

Upper
Gaylor L.

GREAT SIERRA WAGON R.

To Lee
Vining

Granite
Lks.

❻

Tioga Cr.

120

Tioga Pass
Road

❼

Gaylor Peak
11,004'

⑤ P

Tioga
Lake

Middle
Gaylor L.

ALSO SEE MAPS ON
PAGES 14 • 27 • 29

4.

To Tioga Pass entrance

Mine Creek to
Fantail Lake and Spuller Lake

of the mine to market. The trail leads to the abandoned Tioga Mine, shut down in 1884, and to Bennettville. En route, the trail passes a series of meadow-rimmed tarns. Throughout the hike are scenic vistas of Tioga Lake, Mount Dana, the Kuna Crest, White Mountain, Mount Conness, Tioga Peak, and the glacier-encrusted Sierra Crest.

Driving directions: From the Tioga Pass park entrance, drive 1.3 miles east on Highway 120 / Tioga Pass Road to a deep pullout on the left, directly across the highway from Tioga Lake.

From Lee Vining at Highway 395, drive 10.9 miles west on Highway 120 / Tioga Pass Road to the trailhead pullout on the right, directly across the highway from Tioga Lake.

Hiking directions: Head north on the old Great Sierra Wagon Road, passing boulders that close the road to vehicles. Stay left at a road fork and continue through the open lodgepole pine forest. Cross a small rise to an overlook of Tioga Lake and the surrounding peaks. Walk through a grassy meadow, and pass four small, grass-lined lakes dotted with lodgepole and whitebark pines. Cross over another small hill, with Tioga Peak looming over the trail straight ahead. Descend on the rocky path into Mine Creek Canyon to the base of the cliffs. On the left, a waterfall cascades down the 11,000-foot cliffs. A side path veers off to the right and across the meadow to Mine Creek. Directly across the creek on a low ridge are the historically restored buildings of Bennettville. Stay on the main trail straight ahead to the abandoned Tioga Mine tunnel, with a collection of rusted mining equipment, pieces of track, and a pile of tailings. Traverse Tioga Hill, passing the mine, and descend into the meadow, marbled with streams, to Mine Creek. Cross the creek on a log bridge and climb up the small rise south of Shell Lake. Descend to the right to the two remaining Bennettville structures. This is the turn-around spot.

To hike farther, the upstream route leads to Shell Lake, Mine Lake, Fantail Lake, and Spuller Lake (Hike 4). Downstream, the trail returns to Junction Campground by Saddlebag Lake Road.

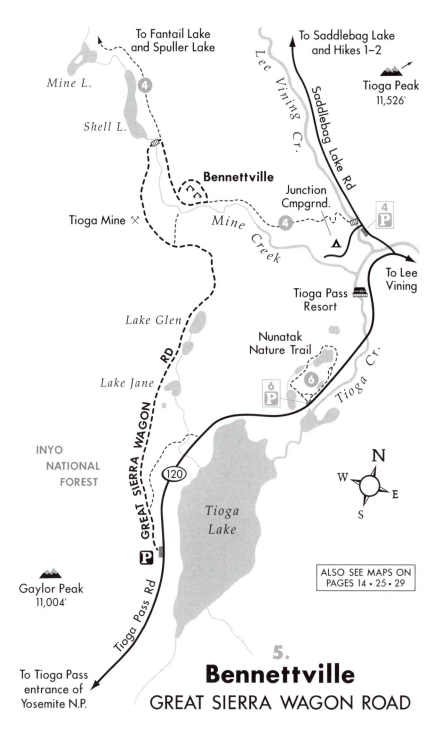

To Fantail Lake
and Spuller Lake

To Saddlebag Lake
and Hikes 1–2

Lee Vining Cr.

Saddlebag Lake Rd

Tioga Peak
11,526'

Mine L.

④

Shell L.

Bennettville

Junction
Cmpgrnd.

Tioga Mine ✕

Mine Creek

④

④
P

To Lee
Vining

Tioga Pass
Resort

Lake Glen

Nunatak
Nature Trail

Lake Jane

⑥
P

⑥

Tioga Cr.

INYO
NATIONAL
FOREST

GREAT SIERRA WAGON RD.

120

Tioga
Lake

N
W   E
S

ALSO SEE MAPS ON
PAGES 14 • 25 • 29

P

Gaylor Peak
11,004'

Tioga Pass Rd

5.
Bennettville
GREAT SIERRA WAGON ROAD

To Tioga Pass
entrance of
Yosemite N.P.

6. Nunatak Nature Trail

Hiking distance: 0.5-mile loop
Hiking time: 30 minutes
Elevation gain: Level
Maps: U.S.G.S. Mount Dana and Tioga Pass

Summary of hike: Nunataks are windswept peaks and plateaus emerging above the ancient ocean of glacial ice. The Nunatak Nature Trail (also known as the Tioga Tarns Trail) is a half-mile interpretive trail with panels describing the treeless islands above the ice, the glacially formed U-shaped canyons, the alpine landscapes, and the vegetation of the surrounding terrain. The trailhead is located along Highway 120 between Tioga Lake and the Tioga Pass Resort, less than two miles outside of the east entrance to Yosemite National Park. The trail circles a hill beneath Gaylor Peak amidst the four Thimble Lakes, glacier-formed tarns at 9,600 feet. Throughout the hike are views of Gaylor Peak, Mammoth Peak, Mount Dana Plateau, Tioga Peak, and the nunataks.

Driving directions: From the Tioga Pass park entrance, drive 1.6 miles east on Highway 120/Tioga Pass Road to the posted, paved pullout on the left.

From Lee Vining at Highway 395, drive 10.6 miles west on Highway 120/Tioga Pass Road, to the posted, paved pullout on the right.

Hiking directions: From the trailhead sign, head away from the road to a junction and interpretive panel. Continue straight, hiking clockwise, and enter the pastoral forest to the north end of a lake on the left. Curve around the hillside to a second tarn, tucked between the hillside on the east and the 10,018-foot mountain on the west. Cross a connector stream, linking the second and third lakes. Follow the east shore of Lake 3, the largest and prettiest of the lakes. Loop around the north end of the lake through lodgepole pines, whitebark pines, heather, and fireweed. The path soon returns to Highway 120. Parallel the road along the east edge of a grass-lined pond, completing the loop.

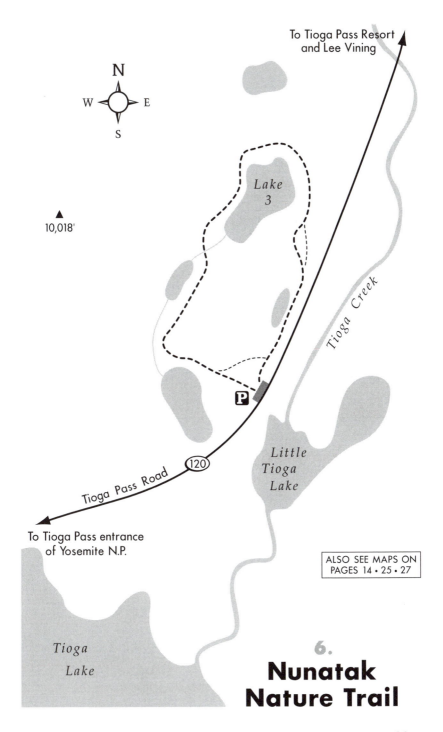

To Tioga Pass Resort
and Lee Vining

N
W ◆ E
S

10,018'

Lake 3

Tioga Creek

P

120

Tioga Pass Road

Little Tioga Lake

To Tioga Pass entrance
of Yosemite N.P.

ALSO SEE MAPS ON
PAGES 14 • 25 • 27

Tioga Lake

6.

Nunatak Nature Trail

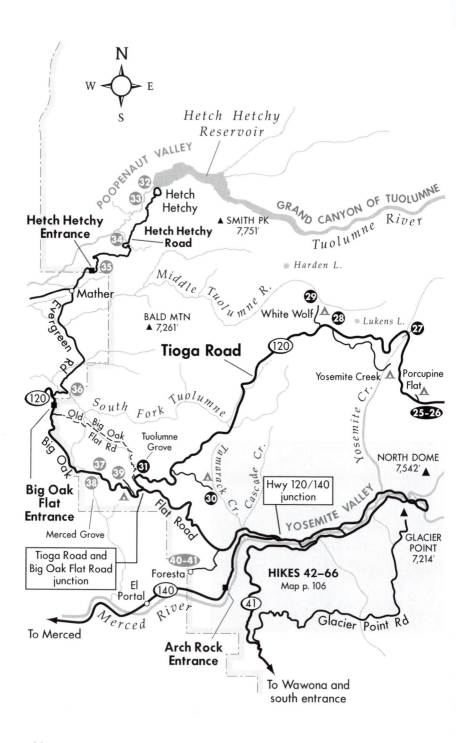

N
W E
S

Hetch Hetchy Reservoir

POOPENAUT VALLEY

32
33

Hetch Hetchy

Hetch Hetchy Entrance

34

Hetch Hetchy Road

▲ SMITH PK 7,751'

GRAND CANYON OF TUOLUMNE

Tuolumne River

35

Mather

● *Harden L.*

Middle Tuolumne R.

Evergreen Rd

BALD MTN ▲ 7,261'

29

White Wolf

28

● *Lukens L.*

27

Tioga Road

120

Yosemite Creek △

Porcupine Flat △

120

36

South Fork Tuolumne

Old Big Oak Flat Rd

Tuolumne Grove

31

25-26

Yosemite Cr.

NORTH DOME 7,542' ▲

Big Oak

37

39

38

Big Oak Flat Entrance

Merced Grove

Tamarack Cr.

Cascade Cr.

30

Hwy 120/140 junction

YOSEMITE VALLEY

▲ GLACIER POINT 7,214'

Tioga Road and Big Oak Flat Road junction

Flat Road

40-41

Foresta ○

El Portal ○

140

HIKES 42–66 Map p. 106

41

Merced River

Glacier Point Rd

To Merced

Arch Rock Entrance

To Wawona and south entrance

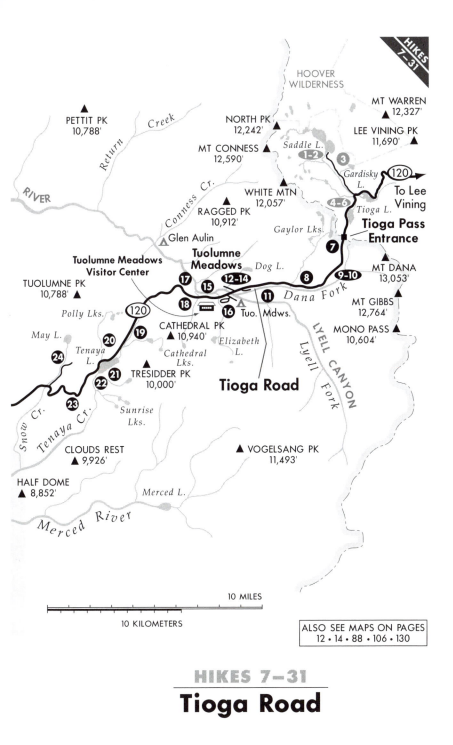

PETTIT PK
10,788'

Return *Creek*

RIVER

NORTH PK
12,242'

MT CONNESS ▲
12,590'

Saddle L.
1-2

3

HOOVER
WILDERNESS

MT WARREN
▲ 12,327'

LEE VINING PK
11,690' ▲

Gardisky
L.

120

To Lee
Vining

WHITE MTN
12,057'

RAGGED PK
10,912'

Conness Cr.

▲Glen Aulin

4-6

Tioga L.

Gaylor Lks.

Tioga Pass
Entrance

7

Tuolumne
Meadows

Dog L.

Tuolumne Meadows
Visitor Center

17

15

12-14

8

9-10

MT DANA
13,053'

TUOLUMNE PK
10,788' ▲

120

18

16 *Tuo.* Mdws.

11

Dana Fork

MT GIBBS
12,764'

Polly Lks.

CATHEDRAL PK
▲ 10,940'

Elizabeth
L.

MONO PASS ▲
10,604'

May L.

19

20

Tenaya
L.

Cathedral
Lks.

Tioga Road

LYELL CANYON

24

21

TRESIDDER PK
10,000'

22

23

Sunrise
Lks.

Snow Cr.

Tenaya Cr.

CLOUDS REST
▲ 9,926'

▲ VOGELSANG PK
11,493'

Lyell Fork

HALF DOME
▲ 8,852'

Merced L.

Merced River

10 MILES

10 KILOMETERS

ALSO SEE MAPS ON PAGES
12 • 14 • 88 • 106 • 130

HIKES 7-31
Tioga Road

7. Middle and Upper Gaylor Lakes

Hiking distance: 4 miles round trip
Hiking time: 3 hours
Elevation gain: 800 feet
Maps: U.S.G.S. Tioga Pass

Summary of hike: Middle and Upper Gaylor Lakes are tucked along the west flank of Gaylor Peak at the Yosemite National Park boundary by Tioga Pass. The hike to the lakes leads up and across a top-of-the-world alpine plateau. The lakes sit above 10,000 feet in a treeless meadow teaming with wildflowers, babbling creeks, rocky knolls, and an endless panorama of mountain peaks in every direction. The hike includes a visit to a stone cabin, built of stacked rock without mortar, and the remains of the Great Sierra Mine, built in the late 1870s. From the mine is a magnificent view south of the two lakes and the surrounding peaks.

Driving directions: From the Tuolumne Meadows Visitor Center drive 8.2 miles east on Tioga Road to the Tioga Pass park entrance. The parking lot is on the left (west) side of the road, 100 feet before reaching the exit station at the park's boundary.

Hiking directions: Pass the interpretive displays and head west, leading uphill through a lodgepole pine forest. The first 0.6 miles is a steep ascent up a rocky trail to a broad, open saddle overlooking Middle Gaylor Lake and the majestic peaks that loom in the distance. Descend 200 feet to the lake. Turn right and closely follow the north shore of Middle Gaylor Lake to the inlet stream that links the middle and upper lakes. Cross the stream and continue north (right) along the west edge of the stream until reaching Upper Gaylor Lake. Stay close to the west shore of Upper Gaylor Lake, backed by the cone-shaped Gaylor Peak, and continue north. Head up the hillside en route to the stone cabin and the Great Sierra Mine at the park boundary, which can be seen above on Tioga Hill. The last 0.2 miles to the buildings is a steep climb. To return, follow the same path back.

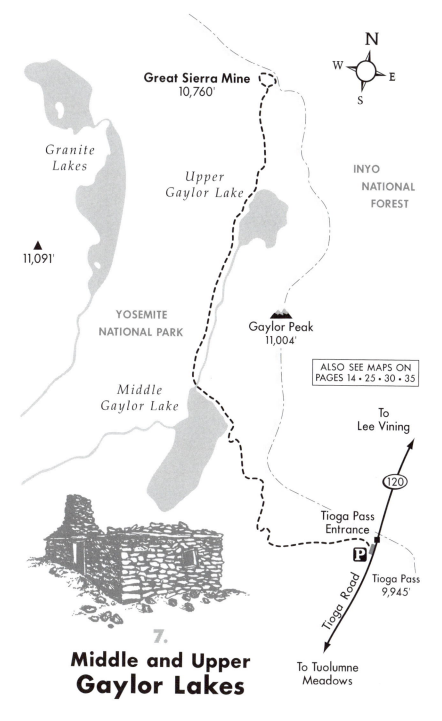

Great Sierra Mine
10,760'

N
W · E
S

Granite
Lakes

*Upper
Gaylor Lake*

INYO
NATIONAL
FOREST

▲
11,091'

YOSEMITE
NATIONAL PARK

Gaylor Peak
11,004'

*Middle
Gaylor Lake*

ALSO SEE MAPS ON
PAGES 14 · 25 · 30 · 35

To
Lee Vining

120

Tioga Pass
Entrance

P

Tioga Pass
9,945'

Tioga Road

To Tuolumne
Meadows

7.

Middle and Upper
Gaylor Lakes

8. Lower Gaylor Lake

Hiking distance: 5 miles round trip
Hiking time: 2.5 hours
Elevation gain: 800 feet
Maps: U.S.G.S. Tioga Pass

Summary of hike: Lower Gaylor Lake is the westernmost of the three Gaylor Lakes. Middle and Upper Gaylor Lakes (Hike 7) are reached from a trail at the Tioga Pass park entrance station. Lower Gaylor Lake, tucked 300–500 feet below the upper lakes, is accessed only four miles from Tuolumne Meadows; a trail connects with Tuolumne Lodge. Lower Gaylor Lake sits in a bowl above 10,000 feet and is bounded by rocky, forested slopes on the north and west sides which rise a thousand feet above the lake. The south and east sides of the lake are open, rock-strewn tundra. The trail climbs through a quiet forest on an easy grade, paralleling the creek to the scenic alpine plateau and lake. This hike mileage begins where the trail crosses Tioga Road. If the hike is accessed from the west side of Tuolumne Meadows Lodge, add an additional 4.6 miles round trip to the hiking mileage.

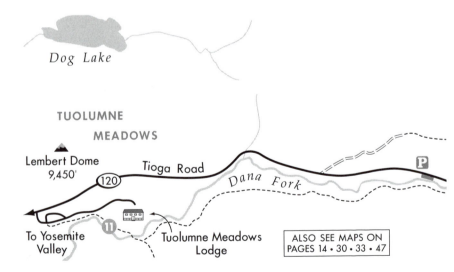

Dog Lake

TUOLUMNE
MEADOWS

Lembert Dome
9,450'

120

Tioga Road

Dana Fork

P

To Yosemite
Valley

Tuolumne Meadows
Lodge

ALSO SEE MAPS ON
PAGES 14 • 30 • 33 • 47

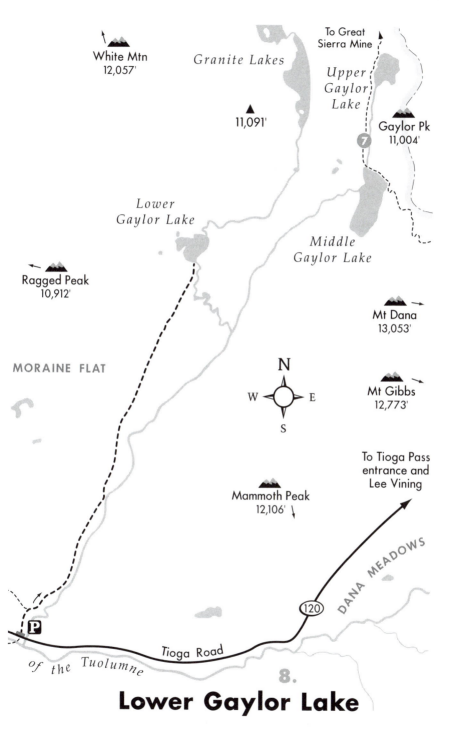

White Mtn
12,057'

Granite Lakes

To Great
Sierra Mine

Upper
Gaylor
Lake

Gaylor Pk
11,004'

7

11,091'

Lower
Gaylor Lake

Middle
Gaylor Lake

Ragged Peak
10,912'

Mt Dana
13,053'

MORAINE FLAT

N

W   E

S

Mt Gibbs
12,773'

To Tioga Pass
entrance and
Lee Vining

Mammoth Peak
12,106'

DANA MEADOWS

P

120

Tioga Road

of the Tuolumne

8.

Lower Gaylor Lake

Driving directions: From the Tuolumne Meadows Visitor Center, drive 4 miles east on Tioga Road to the small, unmarked pullout on the left at the trailhead. The pullout is located 2.4 miles after the posted Tuolumne Lodge turnoff. A wider turnout is located on the right, 0.2 miles before the trailhead.

From the Tioga Pass park entrance, drive 3.9 miles west on Tioga Road to the small, unmarked turnout on the right. The turnout is 2.5 miles after the posted Mono Pass Trailhead parking lot. A wider turnout is located on the left, 0.2 miles past the trailhead.

Hiking directions: Head north, away from the highway and past the trail sign. Walk through the open pine forest with scattered granite boulders on a gentle uphill grade. Curve right, merging with an old unpaved road, and skirt the west edge of a meadow. The outlet stream from Lower Gaylor Lake weaves through the grassland just north of its confluence with the Dana Fork of the Tuolumne River. Steadily climb through the solitude of the forest. At 1.8 miles, emerge from the forest to the open meadows and surrounding peaks, including Ragged Peak, White Mountain, Mount Dana, Mount Gibbs, and Mammoth Peak. Cross the basin directly towards the prominent 11,091-foot mountain peak. Pass a couple of seasonal ponds on the right. The trail ends at the south end of Lower Gaylor Lake by the outlet stream. The lake is fed from above by the Granite Lakes.

For extended hiking, the area can be further explored. However, there are no designated trails. To walk to Middle Gaylor Lake, head east on the open sloping plateau to the middle lake's outlet creek. Continue upstream to the west side of Middle Gaylor Lake. It is one mile to the lake, gaining 300 feet. To reach the Granite Lakes, follow Lower Gaylor Lake's inlet stream from the north end of the lake. This route is also one mile and gains 350 feet to the south tip of lower Granite Lake.

9. Dana Meadows to Mono Pass, Summit Lake, and pioneer cabins

Hiking distance: 8 miles round trip
Hiking time: 4 hours
Elevation gain: 900 feet
Maps: U.S.G.S. Tioga Pass, Mount Dana and Koip Peak

map
page 40

Summary of hike: Mono Pass sits in a saddle between Mount Lewis and Mount Gibbs on the boundary between Yosemite National Park and the Ansel Adams Wilderness. Straddling the 10,599-foot windswept pass is Summit Lake. From the summit are vistas down Bloody Canyon to Mono Lake and the high desert.

Near the summit, a short side path leads to four well-preserved mining cabins from the late 1800s. The abandoned pioneer cabins, remains from the Ella Bloss and Golden Crown mines, are tucked into the northwest foot of Mount Lewis. The hike begins at Dana Meadows and climbs to the alpine pass. For 9,000 years, this trail was a major trading route for the Paiute Indians from the east and the Miwok Indians from Yosemite Valley.

Driving directions: From the Tuolumne Meadows Visitor Center, drive 6.8 miles east on Tioga Road to the trailhead parking area on the right (south) side of the road.

From the Tioga Pass park entrance, drive 1.4 miles west on Tioga Road to the trailhead parking area on the left (south) side of the road.

Hiking directions: Take the wide, well-defined path southeast into the forest. Drop into Dana Meadows, surrounded by Mount Gibbs, Mount Dana, Mammoth Peak, and the Kuna Crest.

Rock hop over braids of Dana Meadows Creek and the Dana Fork of the Tuolumne River above their confluence. Ascend a low ridge, leaving the meadow. Enter a lodgepole pine forest on a gently rolling grade, and climb a series of moraines. Skirt the northeast edge of the meadow along Parker Pass Creek, backed by bald Mammoth Peak. Follow the forested west base of Mount Gibbs, and cross a tributary of Parker Pass Creek to a Y-fork at 2 miles. The right fork leads to Spillway Lake (Hike 10).

To continue to Mono Pass, bear left along the east wall of the valley, staying on the lower slope of Mount Gibbs. Sweeping views span southward to Kuna Crest and Kuna Peak. Curve slightly east and parallel the Summit Lake drainage. Skirt the north edge of a meadow toward prominent Mount Lewis, passing a collapsed log cabin on the right. Less than a quarter mile ahead is a posted junction at 3.4 miles. The right fork leads 1.8 miles to Parker Pass, gaining 500 feet. Stay left and cross an open subalpine slope to an unsigned footpath on the right at the northeast corner of a pond. Detour right on the narrow footpath. Cross the east side of the pond a quarter mile to a group of four historic whitebark pine cabins at  the base of Mount Lewis. Return to the main trail and walk 0.1 mile to the signed 10,599-foot Mono Pass, overlooking Summit Lake. Leave Yosemite National Park and enter the Ansel Adams Wilderness. Continue to the head of Bloody Canyon. This is the turn-around spot.

To hike farther, the trail continues down Bloody Canyon, passing Upper and Lower Sardine Lakes to Walker Lake, 3.5 miles from the pass.

10. Dana Meadows to Spillway Lake

Hiking distance: 7.4 miles round trip
Hiking time: 3.5 hours

map
next page

Elevation gain: 700 feet
Maps: U.S.G.S. Tioga Pass, Mount Dana and Koip Peak

Summary of hike: Spillway Lake sits on a 10,450-foot grassy shelf that is tucked into the base of the towering Kuna Crest. The lake lies in an open bowl west of Parker Pass and Mono Pass beneath numerous 12,000-foot peaks. Parker Pass Creek, a tributary of the Dana Fork of the Tuolumne River, drains from the lake. The trail starts in Dana Meadows and follows the Parker Pass Creek drainage through a meadow marbled with streams to Spillway Lake. The hike shares the first two miles of the trail with Hike 9.

Driving directions: From the Tuolumne Meadows Visitor Center, drive 6.8 miles east on Tioga Road to the trailhead parking area on the right (south) side of the road.

From the Tioga Pass park entrance, drive 1.4 miles west on Tioga Road to the trailhead parking area on the left (south) side of the road.

Hiking directions: Follow the hiking directions to Hike 9 to the Y-fork at 2 miles. The left fork leads to Mono Pass (Hike 9). For this hike, take the right fork, staying in the valley. To the south is a sweeping vista of Kuna Crest, bordered on each end by Mammoth Peak and Kuna Peak. Traverse the west edge of the grassy meadow, paralleling the east side of Parker Pass Creek directly toward Kuna Peak. Descend into and cross the meadow marbled with streams. Enter the forest again, staying close to the cascading creek. Steadily climb between Mount Gibbs on the left and Mammoth Peak on the right. Cross the open tundra in a top-of-the-world landscape towards the cirque of mountains. The trail fades near Spillway Lake at the base of the 11,000-foot cliffs. The open terrain and dramatic vistas encourage exploration.

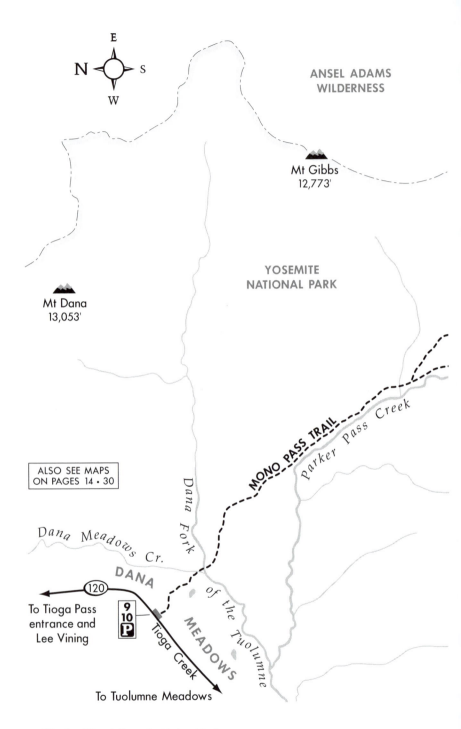

N E S W

ANSEL ADAMS
WILDERNESS

Mt Gibbs
12,773'

YOSEMITE
NATIONAL PARK

Mt Dana
13,053'

MONO PASS TRAIL

Parker Pass Creek

ALSO SEE MAPS
ON PAGES 14 · 30

Dana Meadows Cr.

Dana Fork

of the Tuolumne

DANA

120

9
10
P

To Tioga Pass
entrance and
Lee Vining

Tioga Creek

MEADOWS

To Tuolumne Meadows

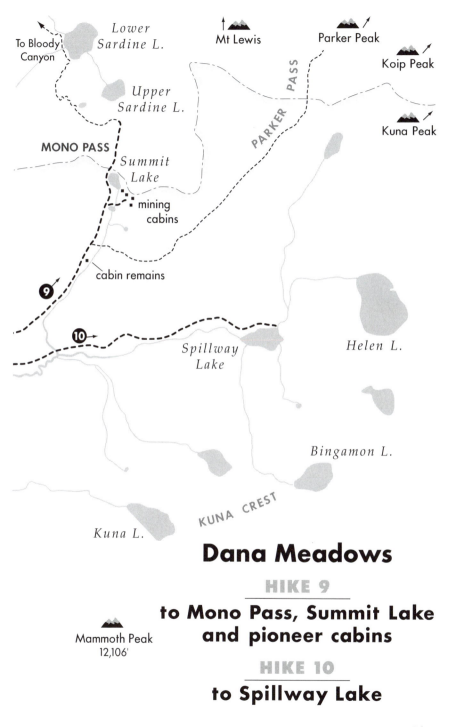

To Bloody Canyon

Lower Sardine L.

Mt Lewis

Parker Peak

Koip Peak

Upper Sardine L.

PARKER PASS

Kuna Peak

MONO PASS

Summit Lake

mining cabins

cabin remains

9

10

Spillway Lake

Helen L.

Bingamon L.

Kuna L.

KUNA CREST

Mammoth Peak
12,106'

Dana Meadows

HIKE 9

to Mono Pass, Summit Lake and pioneer cabins

HIKE 10

to Spillway Lake

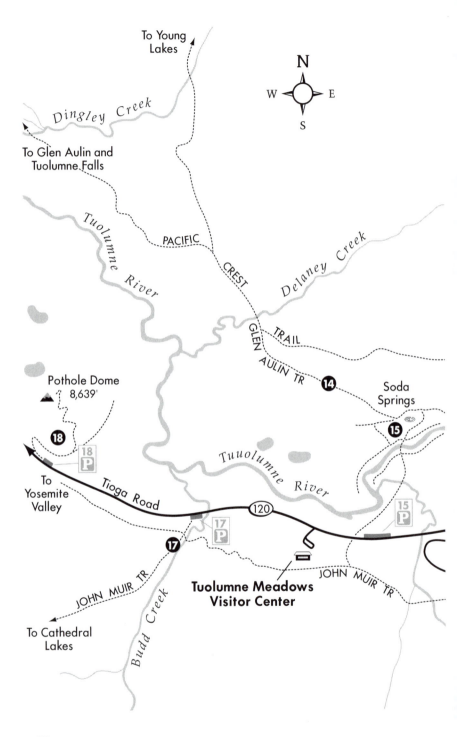

To Young
Lakes

N
W • E
S

Dingley Creek

To Glen Aulin and
Tuolumne Falls

Tuolumne River

PACIFIC

Delaney Creek

CREST

TRAIL

GLEN AULIN TR

14

Soda
Springs

15

Pothole Dome
8,639'

18

18
P

Tuuolumne River

To
Yosemite
Valley

Tioga Road

120

15
P

17
P

17

17
P

**Tuolumne Meadows
Visitor Center**

JOHN MUIR TR

JOHN MUIR TR

Budd Creek

To Cathedral
Lakes

Tuolumne Meadows

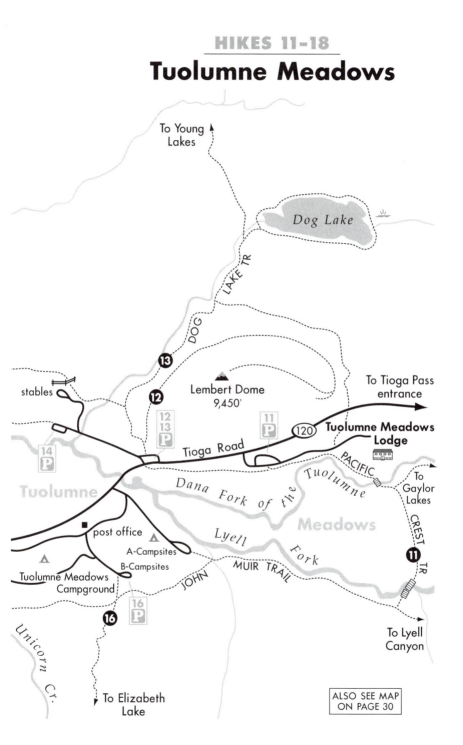

To Young
Lakes

Dog Lake

DOG LAKE TR

To Tioga Pass
entrance

stables

⓭

⓬

Lembert Dome
9,450'

12
13
P

11
P

120 **Tuolumne Meadows
Lodge**

14
P

Tioga Road

PACIFIC

Dana Fork of the Tuolumne

To
Gaylor
Lakes

Tuolumne

post office

A-Campsites

B-Campsites

Lyell Fork

CREST TR

Meadows

⓫

Tuolumne Meadows
Campground

JOHN MUIR TRAIL

16
P

⓰

To Lyell
Canyon

Unicorn Cr.

To Elizabeth
Lake

ALSO SEE MAP
ON PAGE 30

11. Lyell Canyon

Hiking distance: 2.2 miles round trip (or up to 15 miles)
Hiking time: 1 hour or more
Elevation gain: Near level
Maps: U.S.G.S. Vogelsang Peak and Tioga Pass

map
page 46

Summary of hike: Lyell Canyon offers a scenic, pastoral hike along a level section of the Pacific Crest / John Muir Trail. The trail passes through beautiful subalpine meadows along the banks of the Lyell Fork of the Tuolumne River, traveling eight miles before ascending Donohue Pass. Within the first mile, the trail crosses the Dana Fork of the Tuolumne River and a double bridge over the Lyell Fork. The double bridge is built into smooth granite slabs by pools and cascades. This easy, meandering path through gorgeous terrain allows you to hike as short or long a distance as you like.

Driving directions: The trailhead is by the Tuolumne Meadows Lodge parking lot. Drive 1.6 miles east of the Tuolumne Meadows Visitor Center on Tioga Road to the lodge turnoff on the right (south). Turn right and continue 0.4 miles to the first parking lot on the left.

From the Tuolumne Meadows Campground, the hike can be started at the south end of the A-Campsites. The trail parallels the Lyell Fork for one mile to a junction near the double bridge over the Lyell Fork.

Hiking directions: From the lodge parking lot, cross the road to the trailhead. Walk east, parallel to the Dana Fork, and cross the bridge. Follow the forested trail 0.5 miles to the double bridge crossing. Just beyond the bridge is a junction with the John Muir Trail. The trail to the right leads back one mile to the Tuolumne Meadows Campground. Take the trail to the left through lodgepole pines, following the Lyell Fork up Lyell Canyon. A half mile up canyon from the junction is a footbridge that crosses Rafferty Creek. This is the turn-around spot for a 2.2-mile round-trip hike.

To hike farther, the level trail parallels the river through Lyell Canyon for another 7 miles before a steep ascent over Donohue Pass. Choose your own turn-around spot.

12. Lembert Dome

Hiking distance: 2.8 miles round trip
Hiking time: 2 hours
Elevation gain: 850 feet
Maps: U.S.G.S. Tioga Pass

map
page 48

Summary of hike: Lembert Dome is an impressive, polished granite dome with a distinctive profile sculpted by glacial ice. It sits at the east end of Tuolumne Meadows. The dome is named for John Lembert, who built a cabin and raised goats at this site in the late 1800s. From its 9,450-foot exposed dome summit, it offers the premiere view of Tuolumne Meadows and the canyon below. There are sweeping 360-degree views of the surrounding mountain peaks, including Unicorn Peak, Cathedral Peak, Mount Conness, Mount Dana, and Mount Gibbs. The trail up to the north side of the asymmetrical dome is short but steep. Careful footing, especially on the way down, is essential.

Driving directions: From the Tuolumne Meadows Visitor Center, drive 1.2 miles east on Tioga Road to the well-marked Lembert Dome/Dog Lake parking lot on the left (north) side of the road.

Hiking directions: From the parking lot, the trail leads north past the restrooms. At 0.1 mile is a posted trail junction. The left fork leads to Dog Lake—Hike 13. Take the right fork to Lembert Dome. Immediately begin a steep ascent through the lodgepole pine forest around the west flank of Lembert Dome. From the saddle along the north side, the ascent up the bald backside of the dome becomes easier. The climb up the dome is not as steep as it appears from below. There are several levels of the granite dome. Choose your own route as you climb south along the dome's bare, terraced surface. From the first ascent onward are rewarding, spectacular views down canyon. Choose a descending route to suit your own comfort level.

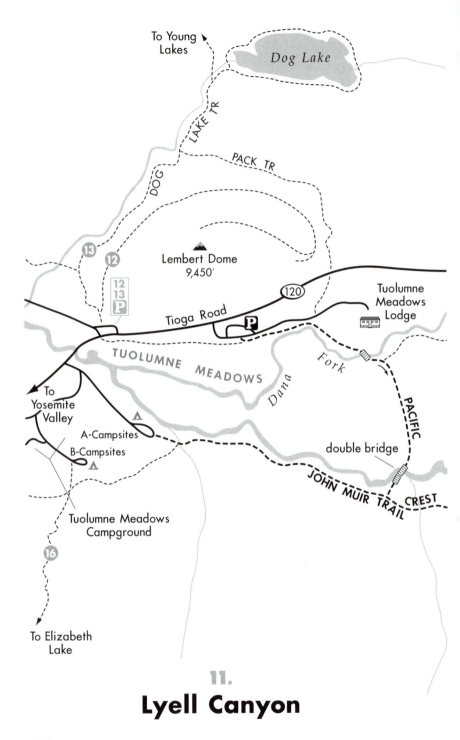

To Young Lakes

Dog Lake

DOG LAKE TR

PACK TR

Lembert Dome
9,450'

120

Tioga Road

Tuolumne Meadows Lodge

P

12 13 P

TUOLUMNE MEADOWS

Dana Fork

PACIFIC

To Yosemite Valley

A-Campsites

B-Campsites

double bridge

JOHN MUIR TRAIL CREST

Tuolumne Meadows Campground

16

To Elizabeth Lake

11.
Lyell Canyon

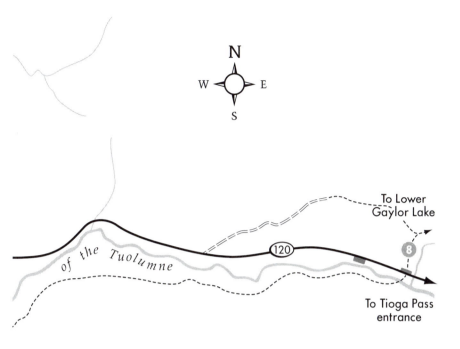

N

W   E

S

To Lower
Gaylor Lake

120

8

of the Tuolumne

To Tioga Pass
entrance

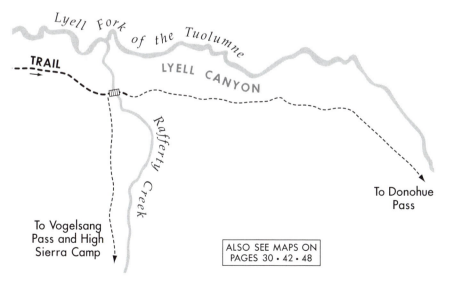

Lyell Fork of the Tuolumne

LYELL CANYON

TRAIL

Rafferty Creek

To Vogelsang
Pass and High
Sierra Camp

To Donohue
Pass

ALSO SEE MAPS ON
PAGES 30 • 42 • 48

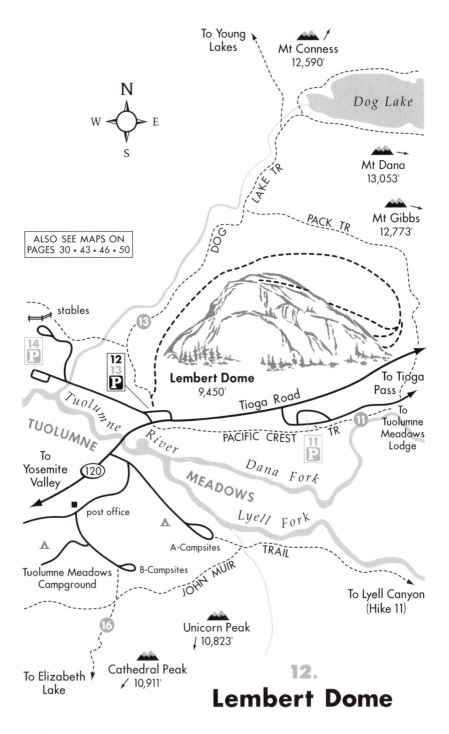

To Young
Lakes

Mt Conness
12,590'

Dog Lake

N
W E
S

Mt Dana
13,053'

DOG

LAKE TR

PACK TR

Mt Gibbs
12,773'

ALSO SEE MAPS ON
PAGES 30 • 43 • 46 • 50

stables

13

14
P

12
13
P

Lembert Dome
9,450'

Tioga Road

To Tioga
Pass

To
Tuolumne
Meadows
Lodge

11

Tuolumne

TUOLUMNE

River

PACIFIC CREST   TR

11
P

To
Yosemite
Valley

120

Dana Fork

MEADOWS

Lyell Fork

post office

A-Campsites

TRAIL

To Lyell Canyon
(Hike 11)

Tuolumne Meadows
Campground

B-Campsites

JOHN MUIR

16

Unicorn Peak
↓ 10,823'

To Elizabeth
Lake

Cathedral Peak
↗ 10,911'

12.
Lembert Dome

13. Dog Lake

Hiking distance: 2.4 miles round trip
Hiking time: 1.5 hours
Elevation gain: 600 feet
Maps: U.S.G.S. Tioga Pass

map
page 50

Summary of hike: Dog Lake, sitting at an elevation of 9,240 feet, is a beautiful half-mile-long lake surrounded by grassy meadows and stands of lodgepole pines. A smooth, level path circles the lake while mountain peaks rise up in the distance. The grassy terrain, pretty surroundings, and eastward views of the Sierra Crest make this an enjoyable place for a picnic. The trail to Dog Lake begins at the east end of Tuolumne Meadows near the base of Lembert Dome. The path leads through a lodgepole pine and fir forest to the alpine lake.

Driving directions: From the Tuolumne Meadows Visitor Center, drive 1.2 miles east on Tioga Road to the well-marked Lembert Dome/Dog Lake parking lot on the left (north) side of the road.

Hiking directions: From the parking lot, the trail leads north past the restrooms to a trail junction. The right fork leads to Lembert Dome—Hike 12. Take the Dog Lake Trail to the left. Head through a small meadow and into the lodgepole forest, passing a trail from the stables on the left at 0.2 miles. From here, the path climbs under the west face of Lembert Dome, gaining over 400 feet in the next half mile. As the trail levels off, there is a stream crossing to another junction. The right fork is a pack trail that leads around the north side of Lembert Dome. Stay left and continue gently uphill to another junction one mile from the trailhead. The left trail leads to Young Lakes, 4.9 miles ahead. Bear to the right, and walk 0.2 miles to the west end of Dog Lake. The designated trail leads along the southern shore, although trails lead around the lake in both directions. The east end of the lake is wet and boggy until late summer. Return along the same trail.

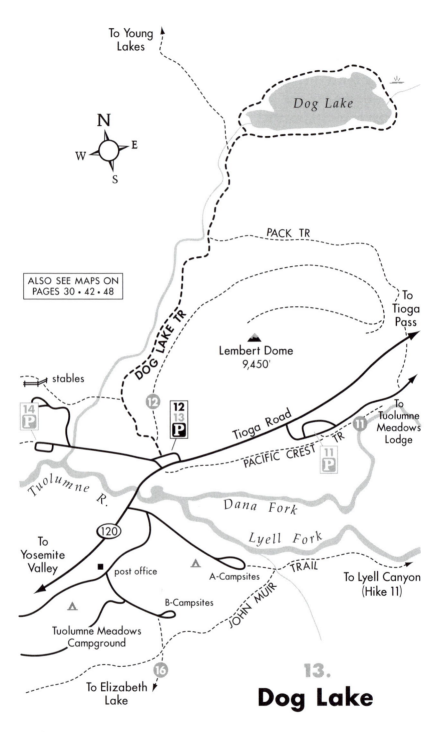

To Young Lakes

Dog Lake

N
W · E
S

PACK TR

ALSO SEE MAPS ON
PAGES 30 · 42 · 48

DOG LAKE TR

To Tioga Pass

stables

Lembert Dome
9,450'

14
P

12

12
13
P

Tioga Road

To Tuolumne Meadows Lodge

PACIFIC CREST TR

11

11
P

Tuolumne R.

Dana Fork

Lyell Fork

To Yosemite Valley

120

post office

A-Campsites

TRAIL

To Lyell Canyon
(Hike 11)

B-Campsites

JOHN MUIR

Tuolumne Meadows
Campground

16

To Elizabeth Lake

13.
Dog Lake

14. Glen Aulin and Tuolumne Falls

Hiking distance: 10.4 miles round trip
Hiking time: 5 hours
Elevation gain: 400 feet
Maps: U.S.G.S. Tioga Pass and Falls Ridge

**map
next page**

Summary of hike: The Glen Aulin Trail, a section of the Pacific Crest Trail, is a popular hike that leads to Glen Aulin High Sierra Camp and the Grand Canyon of the Tuolumne River. This hike follows the Tuolumne River through scenic open meadows to Tuolumne Falls and White Cascade. Beyond the meadows, the trail passes magnificent cascades and waterfalls all the way to Glen Aulin. Tuolumne Falls and White Cascade are a continuous, powerful 200-foot cascade with foaming pools tumbling down a granite slope. From the top of the falls, the path descends along the raging whitewater of White Cascade and ends at a deep river pool and pebbly beach in Glen Aulin.

Driving directions: From the Tuolumne Meadows Visitor Center, drive 1.2 miles east on Tioga Road to the well-marked Lembert Dome/Dog Lake trailhead parking lot on the left (north) side of the road. Turn left and follow the gravel road 0.3 miles to the parking area by the locked gate.

Hiking directions: Take the unpaved road past the trail gate along the north edge of Tuolumne Meadows. Pass interpretive displays to a signed trail split. The left fork stays in the meadow on Old Tioga Road (Hike 15). Take the right fork above the meadow to an overlook of Soda Springs. Bear to the right at the posted Glen Aulin Trail. Enter the forest and cross Delaney Creek on a log to the right of the trail at 1.4 miles. The near-level path skirts a large meadow on the left to a posted Y-fork at 1.7 miles. The right fork leads to the Young Lakes. Take the left fork, reaching the Tuolumne River at the east end of an open, grassy meadow. Views of Cathedral and Unicorn Peaks span to the south. Cross three consecutive branches of Dingley Creek at 2.7 miles. Continue following the meandering Tuolumne River. The trail alternates from meadows to shady forests to bare granite slabs,

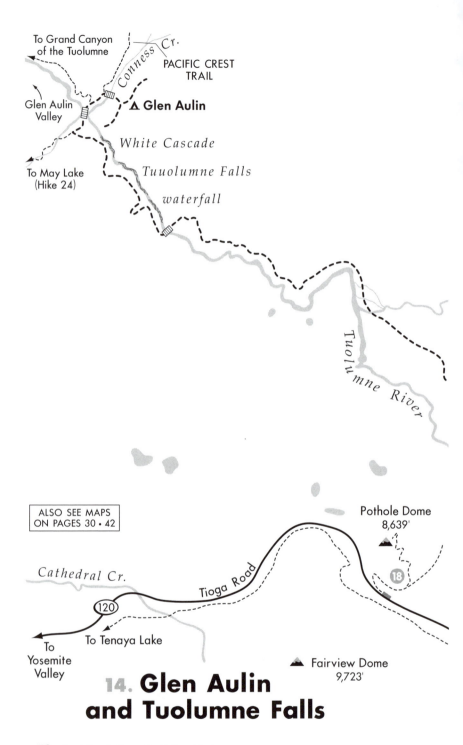

To Grand Canyon
of the Tuolumne

Conness Cr.

PACIFIC CREST
TRAIL

Glen Aulin
Valley

▲ **Glen Aulin**

White Cascade

To May Lake
(Hike 24)

Tuuolumne Falls

waterfall

Tuolumne River

ALSO SEE MAPS
ON PAGES 30 • 42

Pothole Dome
8,639'

Cathedral Cr.

Tioga Road

120

To Tenaya Lake

18

To
Yosemite
Valley

▲ Fairview Dome
9,723'

14. **Glen Aulin
and Tuolumne Falls**

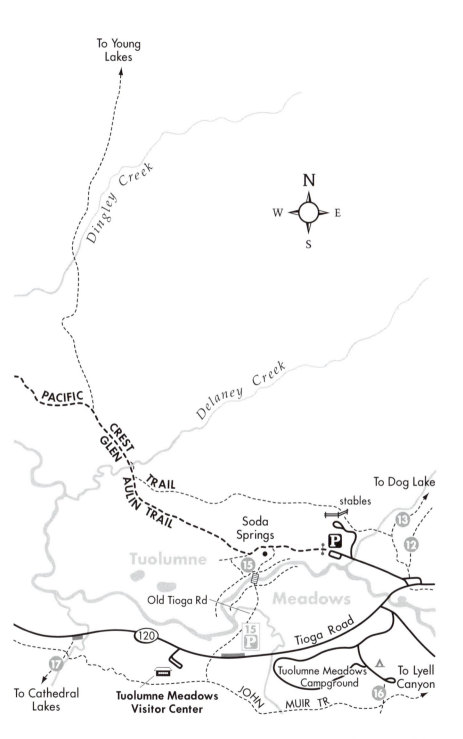

To Young
Lakes

Dingley Creek

N
W E
S

Delaney Creek

PACIFIC

CREST
GLEN

TRAIL

AULIN TRAIL

To Dog Lake

stables

13

12

Soda
Springs

P

15

Tuolumne

Old Tioga Rd

Meadows

Tioga Road

120

15
P

17

Tuolumne Meadows
Campground

To Lyell
Canyon

16

To Cathedral
Lakes

JOHN

MUIR TR

Tuolumne Meadows
Visitor Center

where the route is marked with cairns. Climb around a granite outcrop at the river gorge, and descend to a wooden bridge over the Tuolumne River at 4.1 miles, just upstream from a waterfall. Cross the bridge and follow the west bank of the river to a front view of the raging waterfall. The rock-lined path follows the magnificent cascade to the top of Tuolumne Falls. Dip through glades and zigzag down to the base of the raging 100-foot cataract. Follow the roaring river parallel to White Cascade to the May Lake junction on the left at 5.1 miles. Descend to the right and cross a bridge over the river to a 4-way junction. The left fork leads up Glen Aulin Valley, passing a series of waterfalls to the Grand Canyon of the Tuolumne River. The right fork crosses a wooden bridge over Conness Creek to a beach near Glen Aulin High Sierra Camp. From the beach are views of the entire cascade up to Tuolumne Falls. Return along the same trail.

15. Tuolumne Meadows and Soda Springs

Hiking distance: 1.5 miles round trip
Hiking time: 1 hour
Elevation gain: Level
Maps: U.S.G.S. Vogelsang Peak and Tioga Pass

Summary of hike: Tuolumne Meadows is the largest subalpine meadow in the Sierra Nevada Range. The 2.5-mile-long meadow was formed by a glacier more than 2,000 feet thick. This trail crosses a bridge over the Tuolumne River, which winds through the meadow surrounded by peaks and domes. Soda Springs, located on the north side of the meadow, is a naturally carbonated mineral spring. Pools of mineral water bubble up from beneath the ground. Northwest of Soda Springs is the historic Parsons Memorial Lodge, built entirely from native rock and log in 1915 by the Sierra Club. The McCauley Cabin to its south is a pioneer structure built in 1817 that is currently used as a ranger residence. This lush meadow is a popular area for swimming and picnicking. The whole day can easily be spent exploring and day-dreaming in the meadow.

Driving directions: The trailhead is located 0.1 mile east of the Tuolumne Meadows Visitor Center along the north side of Tioga Road. Parking spaces are available alongside the road.

Hiking directions: From the parking area, the wide trail heads north, directly into the meadow. Continue 0.5 miles to a wooden bridge crossing the Tuolumne River. Across the bridge, continue to the left along the river. A short distance ahead is a junction. Take the trail to the right, leading up to Parsons Memorial Lodge and McCauley Cabin. From the lodge, a trail leads east to Soda Springs and an old wooden enclosure on a grassy knoll. From the springs, head back down to the Tuolumne River and the bridge. Additional trails meander along the river and through the meadow.

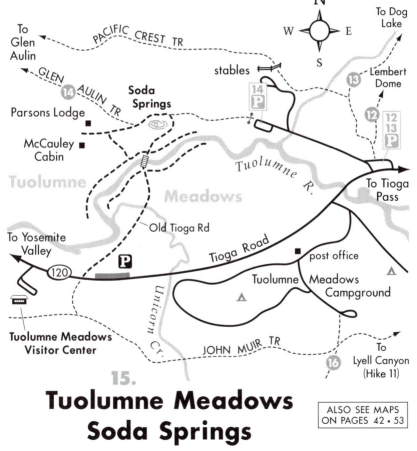

15.
Tuolumne Meadows
Soda Springs

ALSO SEE MAPS
ON PAGES 42 · 53

16. Elizabeth Lake

Hiking distance: 4.6 miles round trip
Hiking time: 3 hours
Elevation gain: 800 feet
Maps: U.S.G.S. Vogelsang Peak

Summary of hike: Elizabeth Lake sits in a gorgeous basin beneath the glacially carved granite cliffs of the Cathedral Range. The dramatic formation forms a cirque around the south end of the subalpine lake, while the spire of Unicorn Peak towers above to the west. The hike to Elizabeth Lake parallels Unicorn Creek, which drains from the lake through a beautiful valley (back cover photo). A lush meadow marbled with streams surrounds the lake. This is a wonderful place to admire the scenery and explore the delicate shoreline.

Driving directions: The trailhead is located inside the Tuolumne Meadows Campground just off Tioga Road, one mile east of the Tuolumne Meadows Visitor Center. At the campground entrance booth, request a free day-parking permit and campground/trailhead map. The trailhead is located by Campsite B-49.

From the Tuolumne Meadows Visitor Center, the John Muir Trail heads east for one mile to the Elizabeth Lake trailhead.

Hiking directions: From the trailhead, head south to a junction with the John Muir Trail, 300 feet ahead. Continue south on the main trail through the shade of a lodgepole pine forest. There is a small stream crossing at 0.5 miles and another crossing at one mile. Just past the second stream, the trail levels off. At 1.2 miles the route meets, then parallels, the cascading waters of Unicorn Creek and emerges into a lush green meadow. The trail divides as it approaches the lake. Footpaths lead in both directions along the picturesque shoreline. After exploring, return on the same path.

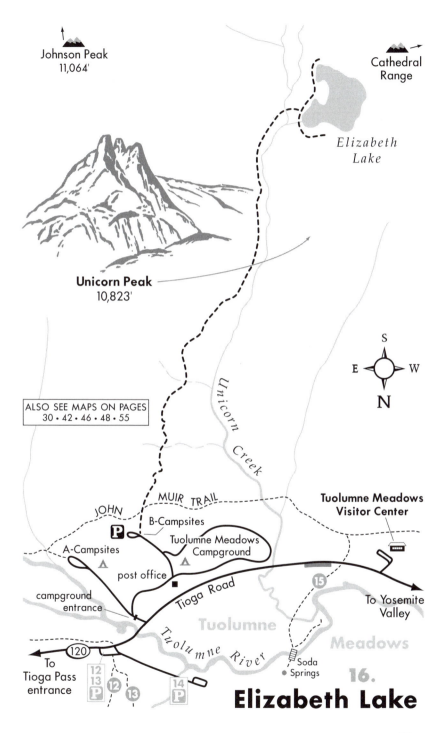

Johnson Peak
11,064'

Cathedral
Range

*Elizabeth
Lake*

Unicorn Peak
10,823'

S

E — W

N

ALSO SEE MAPS ON PAGES
30 • 42 • 46 • 48 • 55

Unicorn Creek

Tuolumne Meadows
Visitor Center

JOHN   MUIR TRAIL

B-Campsites

P

A-Campsites   Tuolumne Meadows
Campground

post office   Tioga Road

campground
entrance

15

To Yosemite
Valley

Tuolumne

Tuolumne River

120

To
Tioga Pass
entrance

12
13
P

12

13

14
P

Soda
• Springs

Meadows

16.

Elizabeth Lake

17. Lower Cathedral Lake

Hiking distance: 7 miles round trip
Hiking time: 4 hours
Elevation gain: 1,000 feet
Maps: U.S.G.S. Tenaya Lake

Summary of hike: Lower Cathedral Lake sits at 9,250 feet in a glacial cirque beneath the horned spire of Cathedral Peak. Glaciated mountains curve around the southwest side of the enchanting lake while bedrock surrounds the lake's perimeter. This subalpine trail up to the lake has views of the Tenaya Lake basin and the smooth, ice-sculpted Fairview Dome. The trail follows a section of the John Muir Trail.

Driving directions: From the Tuolumne Meadows Visitor Center, drive 0.5 miles west on Tioga Road to the trailhead parking lot on the left (south) side of the road.

Hiking directions: From the parking lot, head southwest to a junction at 0.1 mile. The intersecting trail connects Tenaya Lake with Tuolumne Meadows. Continue straight, parallel to Budd Creek. Climb 550 feet through the dense forest in 0.7 miles, then level off for a half mile. Skirt the base of Cathedral Peak's northern granite slope. At 1.4 miles cross Cathedral Creek and begin a second ascent, gaining 450 feet in a half mile. As the trail levels, the route passes through an open, sandy forest while the spires of Cathedral Peak come into full view. At three miles is a fork. The left fork continues along the John Muir Trail to Yosemite Valley, passing Upper Cathedral Lake. Take the right branch to Lower Cathedral Lake 0.5 miles ahead. Zigzag down the rocky slope to a meadow, crossing the outlet stream from Upper Cathedral Lake three times. Several trails cross to the east shore of the lake by flat rock slabs. Choose your own paths to explore. On the west side of the lake are views down the valley to Tenaya Lake and Polly Dome. Return along the same trail.

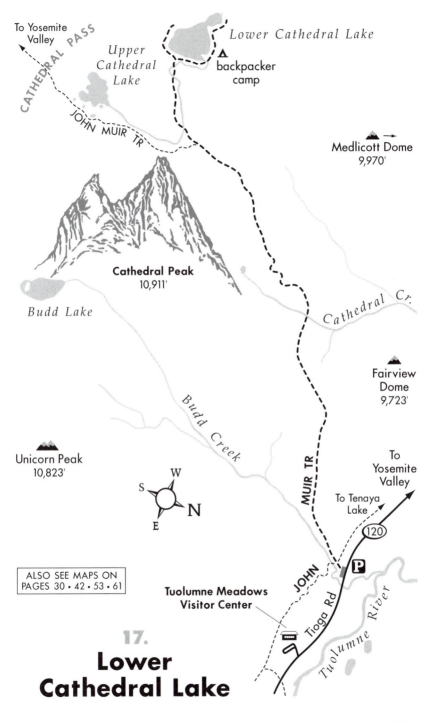

To Yosemite Valley

CATHEDRAL PASS

Upper Cathedral Lake

Lower Cathedral Lake

backpacker camp

JOHN MUIR TR

Medlicott Dome
9,970'

Cathedral Peak
10,911'

Budd Lake

Cathedral Cr.

Fairview Dome
9,723'

Budd Creek

Unicorn Peak
10,823'

MUIR TR

To Yosemite Valley

To Tenaya Lake

W
S
N
E

120

P

ALSO SEE MAPS ON
PAGES 30 · 42 · 53 · 61

JOHN

Tioga Rd

Tuolumne Meadows
Visitor Center

Tuolumne River

17.

Lower Cathedral Lake

18. Pothole Dome

Hiking distance: 1.1 mile round trip
Hiking time: 45 minutes
Elevation gain: 200 feet
Maps: U.S.G.S. Falls Ridge

Summary of hike: Pothole Dome rests on the west end of Tuolumne Meadows. The trail skirts the edge of the fragile subalpine meadow to the trees at the base of the polished granite dome. The hike ascends the smooth and gentle rock slope past erratics, the rounded boulders that were transported and deposited by retreating glaciers. Flowing water trapped beneath the glaciers formed the large and numerous potholes. From the 8,760-foot summit are sweeping vistas of Tuolumne Meadows, the Tuolumne River, Lembert Dome, Fairview Dome, Mount Gibbs, Mount Dana, and the western part of the Cathedral Range.

Driving directions: From the Tuolumne Meadows Visitor Center, drive 1.2 miles west on Tioga Road to the signed pullout on the right (north) side of the road.

Hiking directions: From the west end of the parking area, take the well-defined path along the edge of the meadow. At the west end of Pothole Dome, curve right, looping around the perimeter of the meadow to the base of the dome. Follow the foot of the dome on the edge of picturesque Tuolumne Meadows. At the south end of the dome is a trail split. The main trail continues along the west edge of the meadow. Bear left on the side path to ascend Pothole Dome. Choose your own route up the exposed slope, determined by the gradient you prefer. From the summit are 360-degree panoramic views.

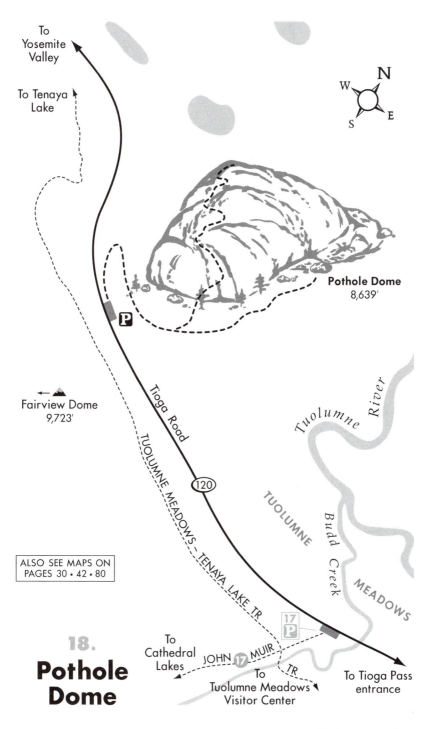

To
Yosemite
Valley

To Tenaya
Lake

N
W
S E

Pothole Dome
8,639'

Tioga Road

Fairview Dome
9,723'

TUOLUMNE MEADOWS - TENAYA LAKE TR

120

Tuolumne River

TUOLUMNE

Budd Creek

MEADOWS

ALSO SEE MAPS ON
PAGES 30 • 42 • 80

17
P

18.

**Pothole
Dome**

To
Cathedral
Lakes

JOHN 17 MUIR

TR

To
Tuolumne Meadows
Visitor Center

To Tioga Pass
entrance

19. Pywiack Dome Falls

Hiking distance: 1.4 miles round trip
Hiking time: 45 minutes
Elevation gain: 200 feet
Maps: U.S.G.S. Tenaya Lake

Summary of hike: Pywiack Dome is a massive 8,651-foot rock formation that rises 700 feet above the northeast corner of Tenaya Lake. The glacier-polished rock sits alongside Polly Dome, which rises a thousand feet higher, visually dwarfing its size. In the mountains to the east of Pywiack Dome are the Cathedral Lakes (Hike 17). The outlet stream from the lakes swiftly tumbles a thousand feet down the steep mountain wall, curving along the southern base of Pywiack Dome before joining Tenaya Creek. Pywiack Dome Falls (not shown on park maps) is a beautiful 30-foot cascade sliding down a huge slab of granite in a narrow drainage. The trail cuts across the base of the granite dome and crosses Tenaya Creek to the falls.

Driving directions: From the junction of Tioga Road and Big Oak Flat Road, drive 33.2 miles east on Tioga Road to the unsigned pullout on the right side of the road. The pullout is located where Pywiack Dome towers over the road, 0.9 miles beyond the picnic area at the northeast end of Tenaya Lake.

From the Tuolumne Meadows Visitor Center, drive 5.4 miles west on Tioga Road to the parking pullout on the left.

Hiking directions: Walk down the sloping granite rock, and head south to Tenaya Creek. Follow the forested path downstream along the west base of Pywiack Dome. At the south end of the massive dome, cross to the east bank of Tenaya Creek. Continue to a wooden footbridge at a half mile, crossing the outlet stream from the Cathedral Lakes just above its confluence with Tenaya Creek. Follow the stream a short distance uphill to the multi-fingered falls, cascading off sloping slick rock at the base of Pywiack Dome. Unmaintained paths lead up to the brink of the falls from both sides of the bridge; the south side is the easiest route.

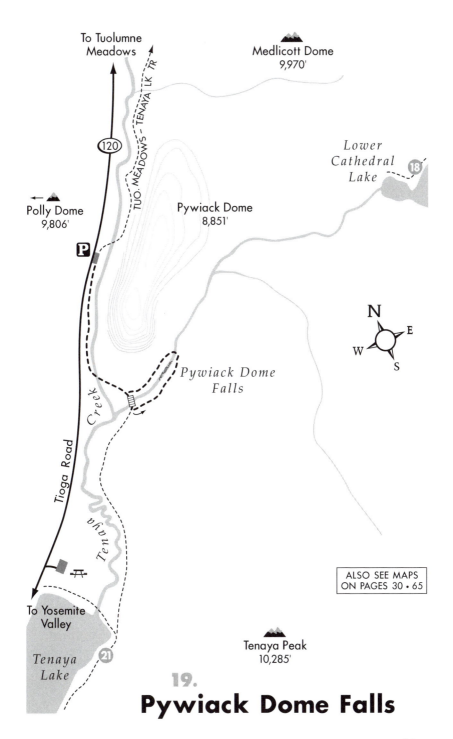

To Tuolumne
Meadows

Medlicott Dome
9,970'

120

Lower
Cathedral
Lake

18

Polly Dome
9,806'

Pywiack Dome
8,851'

P

TUO. MEADOWS - TENAYA LK TR

N
W E
S

Pywiack Dome
Falls

Creek

Tioga Road

Tenaya

ALSO SEE MAPS
ON PAGES 30 • 65

To Yosemite
Valley

Tenaya
Lake

21

Tenaya Peak
10,285'

19.

Pywiack Dome Falls

20. Murphy Creek Trail to Polly Dome Lakes

Hiking distance: 5.5 miles round trip
Hiking time: 3 hours
Elevation gain: 500 feet
Maps: U.S.G.S. Tenaya Lake

Summary of hike: The Polly Dome Lakes lie at the base of Polly Dome, an enormous polished granite dome. The hike begins at Tenaya Lake and parallels the east side of Murphy Creek past Polly Dome. The trail gently climbs through a shady evergreen forest and crosses a series of bedrock slabs peppered with smooth glacial erratics. The last half mile is an off-trail traverse along Murphy Creek to the largest of the Polly Dome Lakes.

Driving directions: From the junction of Tioga Road and Big Oak Flat Road, drive 31.6 miles east on Tioga Road to the day-use picnic area parking lot on the right at the north side of Tenaya Lake. The posted trailhead is directly across the road.

From the Tuolumne Meadows Visitor Center, drive 7 miles west on Tioga Road to the parking lot on the left.

Hiking directions: Cross the highway to the posted Murphy Creek Trail. Enter the Yosemite Wilderness, and climb through the shady lodgepole pine forest. Parallel Murphy Creek, which cascades down a rock slab shelf. At one mile, cross a tributary stream and traverse large granite slabs dotted with glacial erratics. The trail alternates between granite slabs marked with cairns and forested footpaths. At 1.8 miles, cross Murphy Creek on downfall logs. Follow the west bank of the creek upstream to a pond on the right at 2.3 miles. (If you miss the pond, a posted junction to May Lake is a quarter mile ahead.) The pond is also an excellent destination. To continue to the larger lake, rock hop over the pond's outlet stream. Head east, following the watercourse along the base of Polly Dome. The path emerges at the north end of the shallow, boulder-dotted lake. Return along the same path.

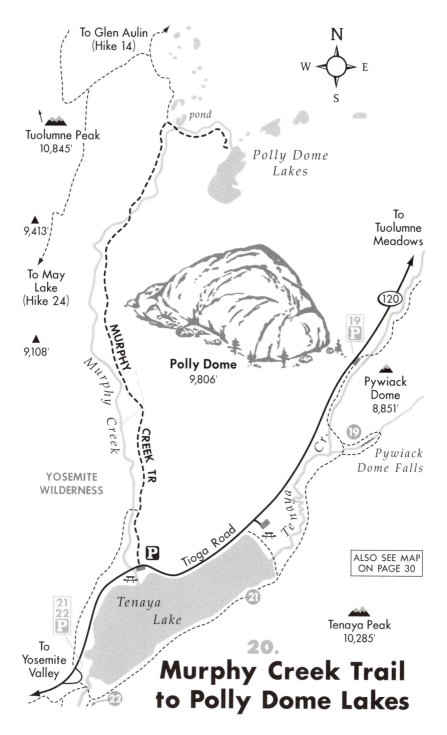

To Glen Aulin
(Hike 14)

N
W E
S

pond

Polly Dome
Lakes

Tuolumne Peak
10,845'

9,413'

To May
Lake
(Hike 24)

9,108'

To
Tuolumne
Meadows

120

19
P

Pywiack
Dome
8,851'

19

Pywiack
Dome Falls

Polly Dome
9,806'

MURPHY

CREEK TR

Murphy Creek

YOSEMITE
WILDERNESS

Tenaya Cr.

ALSO SEE MAP
ON PAGE 30

P

Tioga Road

Tenaya

21

21
22
P

Tenaya
Lake

Tenaya Peak
10,285'

To
Yosemite
Valley

22

20.
Murphy Creek Trail
to Polly Dome Lakes

21. Tenaya Lake

Hiking distance: 2.6 miles round trip
Hiking time: 1.5 hours
Elevation gain: Level
Maps: U.S.G.S. Tenaya Lake

Summary of hike: Tenaya Lake, one of Yosemite's largest lakes, encompasses 150 acres and stretches one mile long. The glacially carved lake lies between the west flank of Tenaya Peak and 1,600 feet beneath Polly Dome, a massive steep-sloped granite rock to the north. This hike circles the oblong lake, passing white sand beaches and picnic areas on the northern shore. The path winds through a remote mixed forest along the southern shore.

Driving directions: From the junction of Tioga Road and Big Oak Flat Road, drive 31 miles east on Tioga Road to the parking lot on the right at the southwest end of Tenaya Lake. Tenaya Lake Campground was formerly located here.

From the Tuolumne Meadows Visitor Center, drive 7.7 miles west on Tioga Road to the parking lot on the left.

Hiking directions: The trail begins at the southwest end of Tenaya Lake. Head east along the campground road towards Tenaya Creek, the outlet stream for Tenaya Lake. After crossing, take the trail to the left, staying close to the south shore of Tenaya Lake. (The trail to the right heads to the Sunrise Lakes, Hike 22.) The near-level trail closely follows the perimeter of the lake through a forest of fir, spruce and pine. At the north end of the lake, reach Tenaya Creek again as it flows into the lake. Cross the creek to the sandy beach along the northeast side of the lake. From the beach, return by taking the same trail back. The views of the surrounding mountains are equally rewarding on the return trip.

For a loop hike, return west on Tioga Road back to the parking lot.

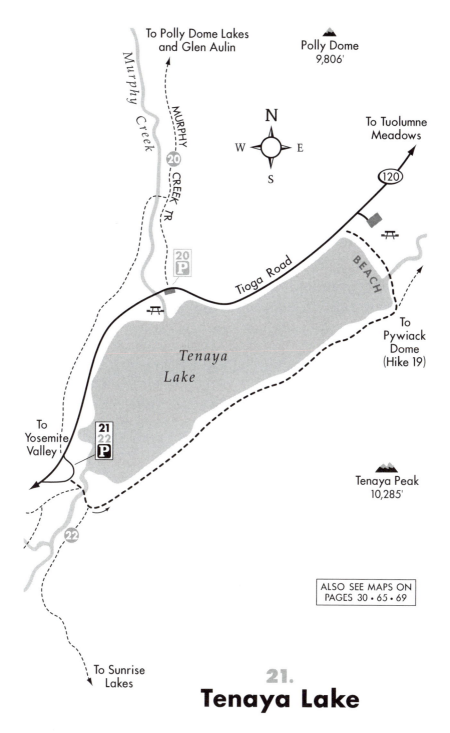

To Polly Dome Lakes
and Glen Aulin

Polly Dome
9,806'

Murphy Creek

MURPHY

20

CREEK TR

N
W   E
S

To Tuolumne
Meadows

120

20
P

Tioga Road

BEACH

+

*Tenaya
Lake*

To
Yosemite
Valley

21
22
P

To
Pywiack
Dome
(Hike 19)

Tenaya Peak
10,285'

ALSO SEE MAPS ON
PAGES 30 • 65 • 69

22

To Sunrise
Lakes

21.
Tenaya Lake

22. Sunrise Lakes

Hiking distance: 8 miles round trip
Hiking time: 4—5 hours
Elevation gain: 1,000 feet
Maps: U.S.G.S. Tenaya Lake

Summary of hike: The Sunrise Lakes are a series of three beautiful lakes beneath Sunrise Mountain. The circular lakes rest at 9,000 feet and drain into Tenaya Canyon. The trail has a steep one-mile ascent on the east slope of the canyon in which most of the elevation gain is achieved. From the ridgetop are dramatic panoramic vistas of Mount Hoffman and Tuolumne Peak, including unique views of Half Dome, Clouds Rest, and Yosemite Valley.

Driving directions: Same as Hike 21.

Hiking directions: The trail begins at the southwest end of Tenaya Lake. Head east along the road towards Tenaya Creek. After crossing, take the trail to the right, descending into Tenaya Canyon through a pine and fir forest parallel to Tenaya Creek. At all the posted trail junctions, head towards Sunrise H.S.C., the high sierra camp located beyond the lakes. At 1.5 miles the trail begins a steep climb out of the canyon, gaining more than 800 feet in one mile via a series of switchbacks. At the crest is a trail junction. Straight ahead leads 4 miles to Clouds Rest. Take a short detour to the right of the junction along an unmarked trail. About 300 yards southwest is a commanding view of Yosemite Valley and Half Dome.

Back at the main junction, take the left (northeast) fork. It is an easy half mile to the first of the Sunrise Lakes, backed by a granite cliff. Wind along the west shore of Lower Sunrise Lake, crossing the lake's outlet stream. Over the next mile, the trail continues gently uphill to the middle and upper lakes. The middle lake is off to the left—a short spur trail leads to the lake. The main trail skirts along the southwest shore of Upper Sunrise Lake, the largest of the lakes and the turn-around point for an 8-mile hike. After exploring, return along the same trail.

To hike farther, the trail continues 1.5 miles to Sunrise High

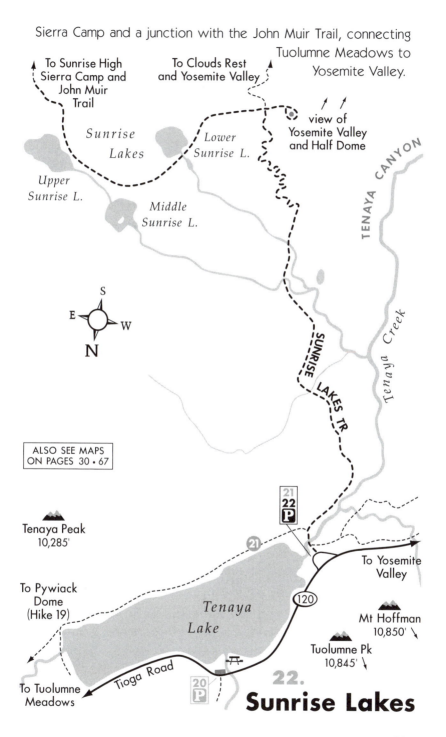

Sierra Camp and a junction with the John Muir Trail, connecting Tuolumne Meadows to Yosemite Valley.

To Sunrise High Sierra Camp and John Muir Trail

To Clouds Rest and Yosemite Valley

view of Yosemite Valley and Half Dome

Sunrise Lakes

Lower Sunrise L.

Upper Sunrise L.

Middle Sunrise L.

TENAYA CANYON

Tenaya Creek

SUNRISE LAKES TR

S
E · W
N

ALSO SEE MAPS ON PAGES 30 • 67

21
22
P

21

Tenaya Peak
10,285'

To Pywiack Dome (Hike 19)

To Yosemite Valley

120

Tenaya Lake

Mt Hoffman
10,850'

Tuolumne Pk
10,845'

Tioga Road

20
P

To Tuolumne Meadows

22.
Sunrise Lakes

23. Olmsted Point

Hiking distance: 0.5 miles round trip
Hiking time: 20 minutes
Elevation gain: 80 feet
Maps: U.S.G.S. Tenaya Lake

Summary of hike: Olmsted Point is on a polished granite dome with scattered Jeffrey pines, lodgepole pines, and glacial erratics. The randomly strewn boulders were left behind after the glaciers retreated more than 10,000 years ago. This short hike begins from a scenic overlook with interpretive panels describing the geological features. The trail leads to an 8,400-foot glaciated knoll with incredible views. The 360-degree scenic vistas extend down Tenaya Canyon to the 9,926-foot Clouds Rest, a rounded back view of Half Dome, Mount Watkins, Polly Dome, Tenaya Lake, the Sierra Crest on the eastern boundary of Yosemite, and the domes and peaks of the Tuolumne Meadows region.

Driving directions: From the junction of Tioga Road and Big Oak Flat Road, drive 29.5 miles east on Tioga Road to the signed parking pullout on the right.

From the Tuolumne Meadows Visitor Center, drive 9.1 miles west on Tioga Road to the parking pullout on the left.

Hiking directions: From the interpretive panel and overlook, take the rock-lined path downhill. Pass large boulders to a signed 4-way junction. The left fork skirts Tioga Road to Tenaya Lake; the right fork leads to Yosemite Valley via lower Tenaya Canyon. Walk straight ahead on the nature trail and curve to the right. Wind through groves of pines, white fir, oak scrub, manzanita and juniper. Ascend the rise and cross a field of erratics to the summit of Olmsted Point on the west rim of Tenaya Canyon. Views down the enormous granite-walled canyon lead to Yosemite Valley. After savoring the surrealistic views of the glacier-scoured landscape, return along the same path.

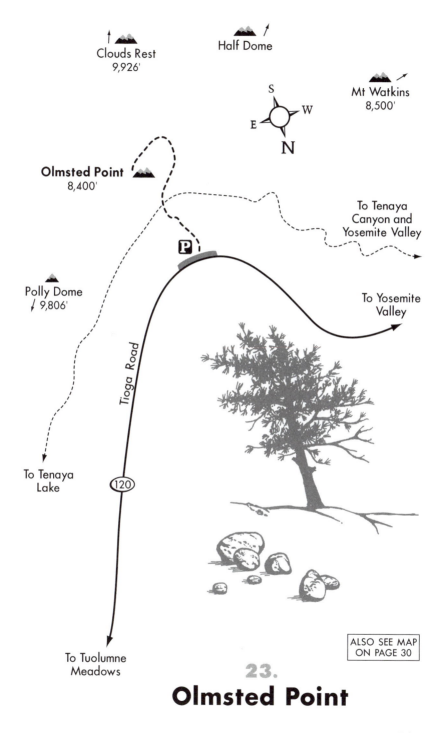

Clouds Rest
9,926'

Half Dome

Mt Watkins
8,500'

S
W
E
N

Olmsted Point
8,400'

To Tenaya
Canyon and
Yosemite Valley

P

Polly Dome
9,806'

To Yosemite
Valley

Tioga Road

120

To Tenaya
Lake

ALSO SEE MAP
ON PAGE 30

To Tuolumne
Meadows

23.

Olmsted Point

24. May Lake

Hiking distance: 2.4 miles round trip
Hiking time: 1.5 hours
Elevation gain: 450 feet
Maps: U.S.G.S. Tenaya Lake

Summary of hike: May Lake is nestled beneath the towering eastern wall of Mount Hoffman, located in the center of Yosemite. The mountain rises more than 1,500 feet out of May Lake to a height of 10,850 feet. The trail offers views of Tenaya Canyon, Cathedral Peak, Half Dome, and Clouds Rest. The forested lake is home to the May Lake High Sierra Camp and is a popular trout fishing lake.

The two-mile road leading to May Lake was a section of the Old Tioga Road, used from 1883 through 1961. It was originally called the Great Sierra Wagon Road and was a supply route to the silver mines on Tioga Pass.

Driving directions: From the junction of Tioga Road and Big Oak Flat Road, drive 27 miles east on Tioga Road to the May Lake turnoff on the left. Turn left and drive 1.8 miles to the trailhead parking lot at the end of the road.

From the Tuolumne Meadows Visitor Center, drive 11.4 miles west on Tioga Road to the May Lake turnoff on the right. Turn right and drive 1.8 miles to the trailhead parking lot at road's end.

Hiking directions: The trailhead is to the left (southwest) of a glacial tarn. Cross the bridge and begin hiking north. The trail steadily gains elevation but is not steep. Pass through an open forest dominated by lodgepole pine and red fir, allowing plenty of sunlight to filter in through the trees. Sections of the trail cross large slabs of granite interspersed with lodgepole pines. Climb over the granite slabs, reaching a saddle overlooking May Lake. Descend to the lake's southern shore. Just before reaching May Lake is a trail fork. The left fork follows the south end of the lake by the backpacker camp. The right fork follows the east side of the lake, passing May Lake High Sierra Camp. After exploring the area, return along the same trail.

To hike farther, the trail continues into the backcountry to the Polly Dome Lakes (Hike 20), northwest to Ten Lakes, and northeast to Glen Aulin (Hike 14).

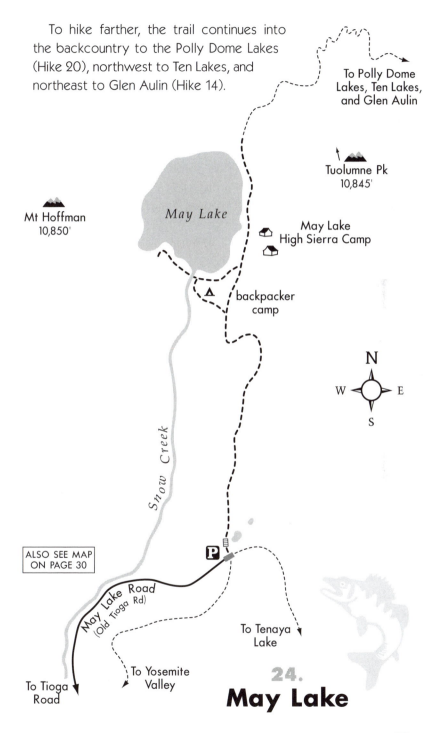

To Polly Dome
Lakes, Ten Lakes,
and Glen Aulin

Tuolumne Pk
10,845'

Mt Hoffman
10,850'

May Lake

May Lake
High Sierra Camp

backpacker
camp

N
W · E
S

Snow Creek

ALSO SEE MAP
ON PAGE 30

May Lake Road
(Old Tioga Rd)

To Tenaya
Lake

To Tioga
Road

To Yosemite
Valley

24.
May Lake

25. Porcupine Creek Trail to Indian Ridge Natural Arch

Hiking distance: 6.4 miles round trip
Hiking time: 3 hours
Elevation gain: 600 feet
Maps: U.S.G.S. Yosemite Falls

map
page 76

Summary of hike: Indian Ridge Natural Arch is a massive, sculpted rock formation with a thin, delicate 20-foot rock arch at its crest. It is Yosemite's only natural stone arch. From the arch, views extend across Indian Ridge to North Dome, Half Dome, Clouds Rest, and the Clark Range. The hike follows the Porcupine Creek Trail through a pine and fir forest to the arch and the great panoramic vistas. For a longer hike, and even better views, the trail continues to North Dome—Hike 26.

Driving directions: From the junction of Tioga Road and Big Oak Flat Road, drive 25 miles east on Tioga Road to the signed parking pullout on the right. It is located one mile past the Porcupine Flat Campground.

From the Tuolumne Meadows Visitor Center, drive 13.6 miles west on Tioga Road to the parking area on the left.

Hiking directions: From the west end of the parking area, take the blocked-off, eroded asphalt road a quarter mile downhill to the end of the pavement. Continue winding through the forest to the former site of the Porcupine Creek Campground. At 0.7 miles, rock hop over a tributary stream of Porcupine Creek, and cross a log over Porcupine Creek to the right of the path. Follow the near-level grade through a small grassy meadow and red fir forest. Rock-hop over another tributary stream to a posted 3-way junction at 1.5 miles. The Snow Creek Trail veers left to Yosemite Valley via Tenaya Canyon (Hike 50). Stay to the right to a second junction 20 yards ahead. The right fork leads to Yosemite Falls (Hike 47). Take the left fork towards North Dome and traverse the hillside. Cross a stream, curve left, and climb the hillside to a saddle on Indian Ridge and a posted junction at just under 3 miles. The right fork leads to North Dome (Hike 26). Bear left and zigzag a quarter mile up the steep hillside path to the natural arch. Curve around the east side of the formation, with views upward of the arch. From the north side of the rock, climb into the window beneath the arch. After savoring the views, return to the Porcupine Creek Trail. Head back to the trailhead along the same route, or continue with Hike 26 to North Dome.

26. North Dome

Hiking distance: 8.8 miles round trip
Hiking time: 4.5 hours
Elevation gain: 650 feet
Maps: U.S.G.S. Yosemite Falls

map
page 76

Summary of hike: North Dome is a 7,542-foot granite promontory on the north rim of Yosemite Valley. From atop the dome are the best close-up views in the park of Half Dome and Clouds Rest. The bald, polished North Dome sits 3,571 feet above the valley bottom, with captivating panoramas of the valley, Tenaya Canyon, Glacier Point, Sentinel Dome, Liberty Cap, Panorama Cliff, and Illilouette Fall. Two routes from Yosemite Valley also access North Dome, but both routes are very strenuous—the Yosemite Falls Trail (Hike 47) and the Snow Creek Trail out of Tenaya Canyon (Hike 50). This hike follows the third and easiest route to North Dome via the Porcupine Creek Trail, which begins from Tioga Road.

Driving directions: Same as Hike 25.

Hiking directions: Follow the hiking directions for Hike 25 to the saddle and the signed junction to the Indian Ridge Natural Arch. Take the trail south towards North Dome. Descend along the crest of Indian Ridge to magnificent views of the surrounding peaks. As you near the ridge's point, the path curves left, descending to North Dome. Before curving downhill, detour straight ahead onto the ridge's nose to a spectacular overlook of North Dome, Yosemite Valley, and close views of Clouds Rest and Half Dome. Return to the trail and leave Indian Ridge, curving east into the forest and returning to the ridgeline below. Follow the ridge south on huge granite slabs, passing to the right of Basket Dome and a signed junction. The right fork leads to Yosemite Falls (Hike 47). Stay to the left and descend rock steps to the base of North Dome. Ascend the bare rock dome to the rounded summit of North Dome. Just beyond the summit are incredible views of Yosemite's granite monoliths, rounded domes, towering pinnacles, and merging canyons. Return along the same trail.

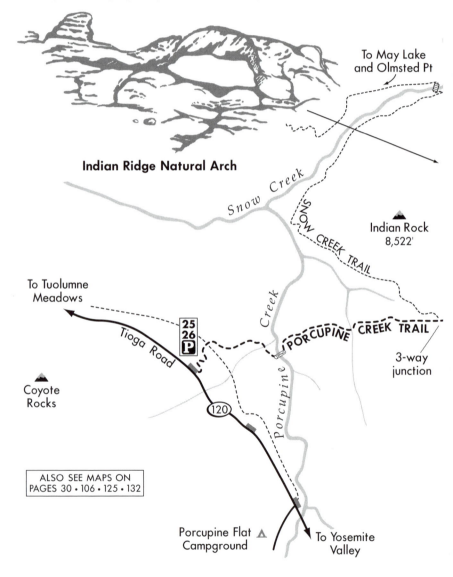

Indian Ridge Natural Arch

To May Lake and Olmsted Pt

Snow Creek

SNOW CREEK TRAIL

▲ Indian Rock 8,522'

To Tuolumne Meadows

Tioga Road

25 26 P

Creek

PORCUPINE CREEK TRAIL

3-way junction

▲ Coyote Rocks

120

Porcupine

ALSO SEE MAPS ON
PAGES 30 • 106 • 125 • 132

Porcupine Flat ▲ Campground

To Yosemite Valley

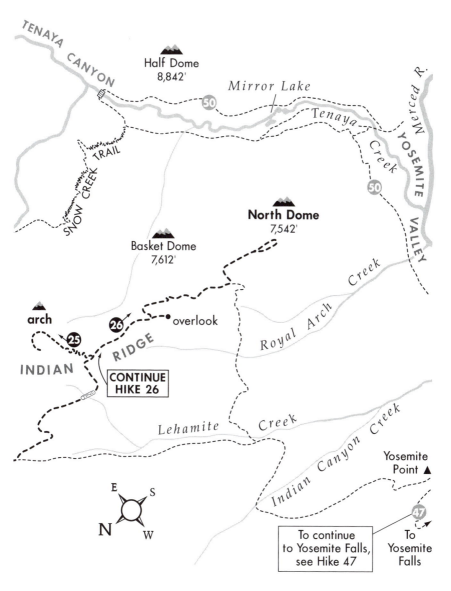

Half Dome
8,842'

Mirror Lake

50

Tenaya

Merced R.

Creek

YOSEMITE VALLEY

50

SNOW CREEK TRAIL

North Dome
7,542'

Basket Dome
7,612'

arch

25

26

overlook

RIDGE

INDIAN

CONTINUE
HIKE 26

Royal Arch Creek

Lehamite Creek

Indian Canyon Creek

Yosemite
Point ▲

47

E S

N W

To continue
to Yosemite Falls,
see Hike 47

To
Yosemite
Falls

HIKES 25 • 26
Porcupine Creek Trail to
Indian Ridge Natural Arch
North Dome

27. Yosemite Creek Trail
from TIOGA ROAD to YOSEMITE CREEK CAMPGROUND

Hiking distance: 4.8 miles round trip
Hiking time: 2.5 hours
Elevation gain: 400 feet
Maps: U.S.G.S. Yosemite Falls

Summary of hike: The Yosemite Creek Trail follows Yosemite Creek from Tioga Road to the viewpoint at the brink of Yosemite Falls (Hike 47), a distance of eight miles. This gentle hike follows the first 2.4 miles of the trail, which descends through a gorgeous, open lodgepole pine forest to a bridge crossing Yosemite Creek. The wide path parallels the creek, following an easy grade to the north end of Yosemite Creek Campground.

Driving directions: From the junction of Tioga Road and Big Oak Flat Road, drive 19.6 miles east on Tioga Road to the large parking turnout on the right. It is 5.1 miles past the turnoff to White Wolf Campground.

From the Tuolumne Meadows Visitor Center, drive 19 miles west on Tioga Road to the parking turnout on the left. It is located 4.4 miles past the Porcupine Flat Campground.

Hiking directions: Walk 80 yards west on Tioga Road to the signed trail on the left. Cross a tributary stream and head into the lush forest. Gradually descend down the trail while meandering past glacier-carved slabs of granite. Pass a pond on the right, and zigzag down to Yosemite Creek at 0.8 miles. Cross the creek on a downfall log or wade across. (Eight miles ahead, this same creek plunges over Yosemite Falls.) Continue south across a trickling stream, and arrive back at the banks of Yosemite Creek alongside a steep granite wall. Parallel the clear creek downstream. Ascend a hill, moving away from the creek, and drop into the upper end of Yosemite Creek Campground at 1.8 miles. Follow the campground road along the creek 0.6 miles to two consecutive bridge crossings and a signed trail on the left. This is the turnaround spot.

To hike farther, the trail continues another 5.6 miles to Yosemite Falls, paralleling the creek for nearly the entire distance.

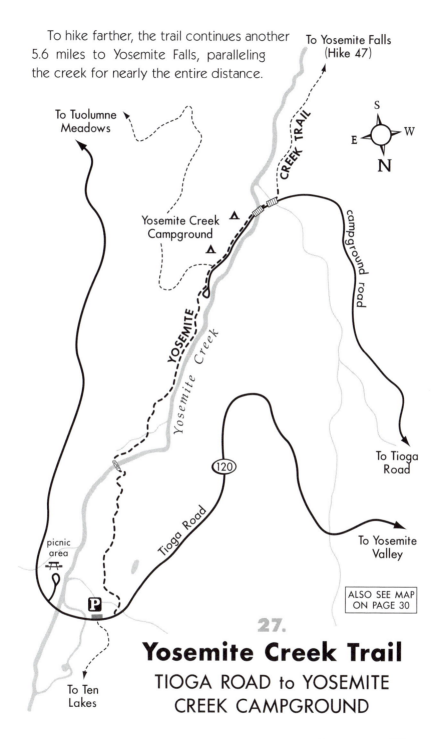

To Yosemite Falls (Hike 47)

To Tuolumne Meadows

CREEK TRAIL

S

E — W

N

Yosemite Creek Campground

YOSEMITE

Yosemite Creek

campground road

120

To Tioga Road

Tioga Road

To Yosemite Valley

picnic area

P

To Ten Lakes

ALSO SEE MAP ON PAGE 30

27.

Yosemite Creek Trail
TIOGA ROAD to YOSEMITE CREEK CAMPGROUND

28. Harden Lake

Hiking distance: 6 miles round trip
Hiking time: 3 hours
Elevation gain: 450 feet
Maps: U.S.G.S. Tamarack Flat and Hetch Hetchy Reservoir

map
page 82

Summary of hike: The trail to Harden Lake follows the original Tioga Road built in 1883. It was closed to vehicles in 1961 when the current Tioga Road was completed. The hike parallels the Middle Fork of the Tuolumne River downstream through a beautiful pine forest past small cascades and pools. Nine-acre Harden Lake, at an elevation of 7,600 feet, is a well-known but uncrowded fishing and picnicking spot.

Driving directions: From the junction of Tioga Road and Big Oak Flat Road, drive 14.5 miles east on Tioga Road to the White Wolf Campground turnoff on the left. Turn left and drive one mile to the White Wolf Lodge. Park near the lodge.

From the Tuolumne Meadows Visitor Center, drive 24 miles west on Tioga Road to the White Wolf Campground turnoff and turn right.

Hiking directions: From White Wolf Lodge, walk down the road to the north, passing the campground. The road (no longer accessible to vehicles) crosses a bridge over the Middle Fork of the Tuolumne River. For the next mile the trail gradually descends, staying parallel to the east bank of the river. At 1.6 miles, a posted footpath to Harden Lake branches off to the right. The footpath crosses the slope of a glacial moraine through a forest of pine, fir and aspen. Either stay on the road or take the footpath. The two routes connect 0.7 miles ahead. (On the road there is a trail fork to the left that is 0.3 miles past the footpath junction—continue on the road.) After the two routes merge, follow the old road another quarter mile to a posted junction to Harden Lake. The left trail continues along the original Tioga Road to Smith Meadow and Hetch Hetchy Road. Instead, take the right fork to the south end of Harden Lake and a trail split. Explore the perimeter of the lake on various side paths. Return along the same route.

To hike farther, the main trail curves to the east side of the lake and steeply descends for several miles into the Grand Canyon of the Tuolumne River. The trail follows along the canyon bottom, eventually leading to Glen Aulin and Tuolumne Meadows.

29. Lukens Lake

Hiking distance: 4.6 miles round trip from White Wolf Lodge
1.6 miles round trip from Tioga Road
Hiking time: 2.5 hours or 1 hour
Elevation gain: 250 feet or 150 feet
Maps: U.S.G.S. Tamarack Flat and Yosemite Falls

**map
page 82**

Summary of hike: Lukens Lake is a scenic mountain lake with forests along one side and beautiful meadows covered in wildflowers along the other. Two routes access the lake. Both trails are easy hikes that lead through lush forests. The longer route begins at White Wolf Lodge. The shorter route begins along Tioga Road.

Driving directions: To start from White Wolf Lodge, follow the same driving directions as Hike 28, parking near the lodge.

The trailhead for the shorter hike is on Tioga Road—1.8 miles east of the White Wolf turnoff. Park on the south side of the road.

From the Tuolumne Meadows Visitor Center, drive 22 miles west on Tioga Road to the trailhead on the left (south) side of the road.

Hiking directions: WHITE WOLF LODGE. The posted trailhead at White Wolf is directly across the road from the lodge. Head east through a lodgepole pine forest along the south edge of the campground. At 0.7 miles is a log crossing over the Middle Fork of the Tuolumne River. At 0.9 miles is a posted trail junction. The trail to the left leads to Harden Lake. Take the right fork, which parallels the river for the next mile, to another junction. The left

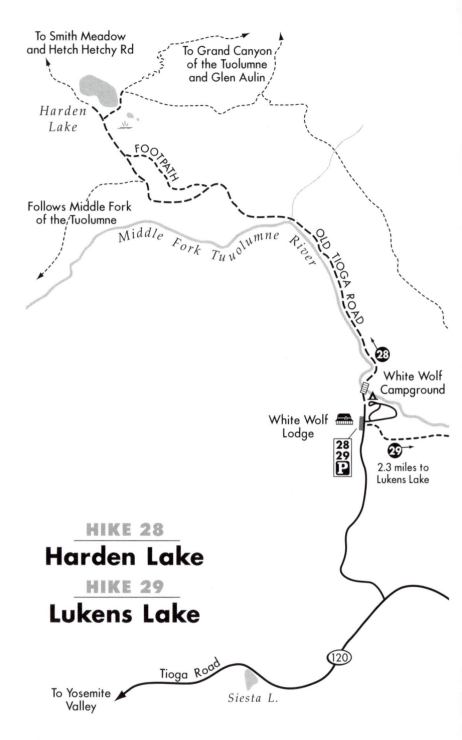

To Smith Meadow
and Hetch Hetchy Rd

To Grand Canyon
of the Tuolumne
and Glen Aulin

*Harden
Lake*

FOOTPATH

Follows Middle Fork
of the Tuolumne

Middle Fork Tuolumne River

OLD TIOGA ROAD

28

White Wolf
Campground

White Wolf
Lodge

**28
29
P**

29

2.3 miles to
Lukens Lake

HIKE 28
Harden Lake

HIKE 29
Lukens Lake

120

Tioga Road

To Yosemite
Valley

Siesta L.

fork continues along the Middle Fork to Ten Lakes. Instead, take the right fork and ford the Middle Fork. Continue uphill to the north shore of Lukens Lake. The trail parallels the lake along the east shore, then leads down to the trailhead on Tioga Road.

TIOGA ROAD. From the pullout on Tioga Road, the trail heads north from the highway through a white pine and red fir forest to a saddle. Descend toward a wet meadow at the south end of Lukens Lake, joining the longer trail from the west.

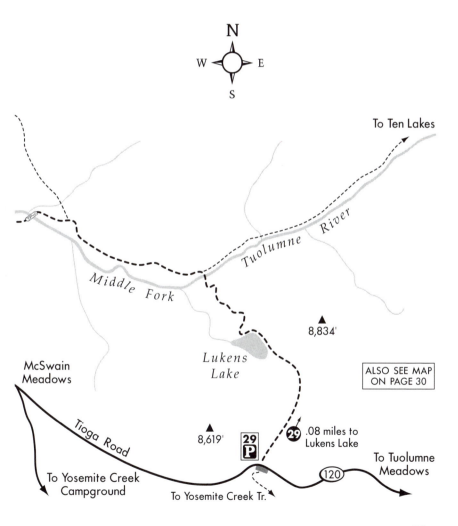

30. Cascade Creek from Tamarack Campground

Hiking distance: 5 miles round trip
Hiking time: 2.5 hours
Elevation gain: 350 feet
Maps: U.S.G.S. Tamarack Flat and El Capitan

Summary of hike: The trail to Cascade Creek is a quiet, secluded hike along the original Big Oak Flat Road that led to Yosemite Valley starting in 1874. The abandoned road has been closed to vehicles since landslides blocked its path in 1942. The trail passes through a mixed evergreen forest and a stunning boulder field to a bridge crossing Cascade Creek.

Driving directions: From the junction of Tioga Road and Big Oak Flat Road, drive 3.7 miles east on Tioga Road to the Tamarack Campground turnoff on the right. Turn right and drive 3 miles to the end of the unmaintained road. Park where a space is available.

From the Tuolumne Meadows Visitor Center, drive 34.8 miles west on Tioga Road to the Tamarack Campground turnoff on the left.

Hiking directions: The trailhead is at the south end of the campground. Walk past the gate to the old abandoned asphalt road that leads through the forest. At 0.5 miles, cross a tributary of Tamarack Creek. At one mile the trail begins its descent. The display of boulders in this area is magnificent. Cross a tributary of Cascade Creek, then follow it downstream to the bridge crossing Cascade Creek. There are numerous cascades along the creek before reaching the bridge—the turn-around spot. One mile below the bridge, Tamarack and Cascade Creeks merge. Just below their confluence, the creek tumbles 500 feet in a long cascade called The Cascades (Hike 42).

To hike farther, the El Capitan Trail continues east to the summit of El Capitan at 8 miles and on to Yosemite Point and North Dome.

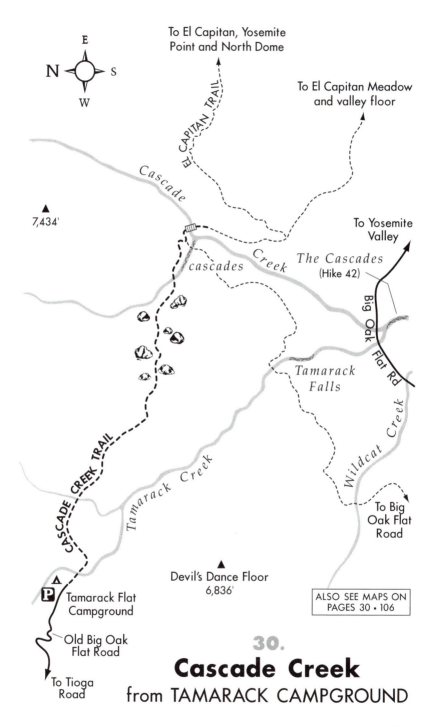

N E S W

To El Capitan, Yosemite Point and North Dome

To El Capitan Meadow and valley floor

EL CAPITAN TRAIL

Cascade Creek

▲ 7,434'

cascades

To Yosemite Valley

The Cascades (Hike 42)

Big Oak Flat Rd

Tamarack Falls

CASCADE CREEK TRAIL

Tamarack Creek

Wildcat Creek

To Big Oak Flat Road

▲ Devil's Dance Floor 6,836'

ALSO SEE MAPS ON PAGES 30 • 106

Ⓟ Tamarack Flat Campground

Old Big Oak Flat Road

To Tioga Road

30.
Cascade Creek
from TAMARACK CAMPGROUND

31. Tuolumne Grove of Giant Sequoias
OLD BIG OAK FLAT ROAD

Hiking distance: 2.5 miles round trip
Hiking time: 1.5 hours
Elevation gain: 500 feet
Maps: U.S.G.S. Ackerson Mountain

Summary of hike: This hike follows part of the Old Big Oak Flat Road that was closed to vehicles in 1993. The historic six-mile section (first constructed in 1874) was part of the road that connected the Big Oak Flat Entrance with Yosemite Valley. Now a hiking trail, the winding road descends through an intimate old forest of incense cedar, sugar pine, white fir, and Douglas fir, reaching the Tuolumne Grove of giant sequoias at one mile. A nature trail begins at the picnic area, once used as a parking lot for viewing the trees. The half-mile trail with interpretive panels loops through the grove of 25 giant sequoias. Included is a walk through the Tunnel Tree (also called Dead Giant), a dead but standing tree trunk that was tunneled for horse-drawn wagons in 1878.

Driving directions: From the junction of Tioga Road and Big Oak Flat Road, drive 0.5 miles eastbound on Tioga Road to the signed parking lot on the left.

Hiking directions: Pass through the trail gate at the far north end of the parking lot, and take the old road into the dense forest. The serpentine road steadily winds downhill through the old-growth forest. At one mile the trail enters the Tuolumne Grove. A short distance ahead is a trail split. On the left is a massive sequoia with a viewing deck. Take the upper trail to the right, passing groves of giant sequoias on both sides of the path. Walk through the dead but standing Tunnel Tree. The two trails rejoin at a nature trail loop by the old parking lot. Bear right on the nature trail, and cross a footbridge over the stream. The path follows the 200-foot length of the downed Leaning Tower Tree. Interpretive displays describe the life of these amazing trees.

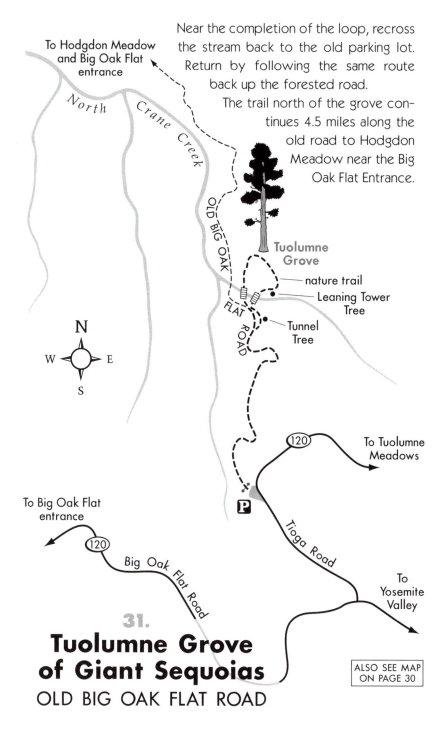

Near the completion of the loop, recross the stream back to the old parking lot. Return by following the same route back up the forested road.

The trail north of the grove continues 4.5 miles along the old road to Hodgdon Meadow near the Big Oak Flat Entrance.

To Hodgdon Meadow and Big Oak Flat entrance

North Crane Creek

OLD BIG OAK FLAT ROAD

Tuolumne Grove

nature trail

Leaning Tower Tree

Tunnel Tree

N
W E
S

120

To Tuolumne Meadows

To Big Oak Flat entrance

120

Big Oak Flat Road

Tioga Road

To Yosemite Valley

31.

Tuolumne Grove of Giant Sequoias
OLD BIG OAK FLAT ROAD

ALSO SEE MAP
ON PAGE 30

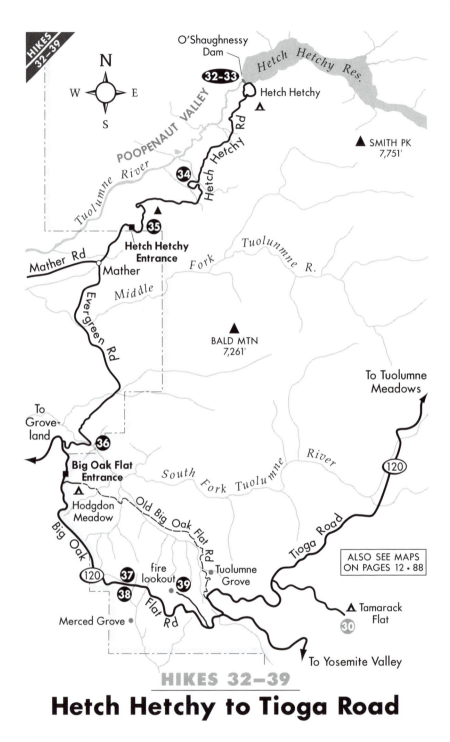

N

W   E

S

O'Shaughnessy Dam

32-33

Hetch Hetchy Res.

Hetch Hetchy

▲

POOPENAUT VALLEY

▲ SMITH PK 7,751'

Hetch Hetchy Rd

Tuolumne River

34

▲

35

Hetch Hetchy Entrance

Mather Rd

Mather

Fork

Tuolumnne R.

Middle

Evergreen Rd

▲ BALD MTN 7,261'

To Tuolumne Meadows

To Grove- land

36

120

Big Oak Flat Entrance

▲

Hodgdon Meadow

South Fork Tuolumne River

Old Big Oak Flat Rd

Tioga Road

ALSO SEE MAPS ON PAGES 12 • 88

Big Oak

120

37

fire lookout

Tuolumne Grove

38

39

Flat Rd

▲ Tamarack Flat

30

Merced Grove •

To Yosemite Valley

HIKES 32–39

Hetch Hetchy to Tioga Road

32. Wapama Falls
from O'SHAUGHNESSY DAM at HETCH HETCHY RESERVOIR

Hiking distance: 4.8 miles round trip
Hiking time: 2.5 hours
Elevation gain: 300 feet
Maps: U.S.G.S. Lake Eleanor

map
next page

Summary of hike: The Hetch Hetchy Valley sits near the western corner of Yosemite, submerged under the Hetch Hetchy Reservoir since 1923. Backed up by O'Shaughnessy Dam, the Tuolumne River now floods the Valley. The dam was built between 1919 and 1923 to provide a water supply to San Francisco. It raised the water level 400 feet above the riverbed, which extends up the glacially carved valley more than eight miles. The hike to Wapama Falls begins from O'Shaughnessy Dam at the west end of the reservoir. A well-maintained trail follows the reservoir's north shore. The trail passes the 1,000-foot wispy ribbon of seasonal Tueeulala Falls en route to the base of the wide and thick Wapama Falls on Falls Creek. The thundering whitewater of Wapama Falls plummets 1,400 feet over a granite precipice and tumbles into the reservoir. Watch for rattlesnakes along the trail.

Driving directions: From the Big Oak Flat entrance station on Highway 120, drive one mile west (outside the park) to Evergreen Road, the first turnoff on the right. Turn right and continue 7.4 miles to a T-junction at the end of the road. Turn right on Hetch Hetchy Road, and drive 1.3 miles to the Hetch Hetchy entrance station. Enter the park and continue 8 miles to a one-way loop at the end of the road. The parking area is at the far end of the loop, just past O'Shaughnessy Dam.

Hiking directions: Walk downhill to the dam, crossing an overlook of the Hetch Hetchy Reservoir. Wapama Falls, the destination of this hike, can be seen from the trailhead to the left of Hetch Hetchy Dome. Cross the top of O'Shaughnessy Dam. Walk through a 500-foot tunnel, carved through the granite mountain, to the posted Hetch Hetchy trailhead. The wide path (an abandoned road) winds along the western edge of the reservoir, following the contours of the mountains. The path gains elevation to magnificent vistas of the reservoir and sculpted mountains. At 0.9 miles is a posted junction. The left fork climbs the mountain to Laurel Lake, 7.6 miles ahead. Take the right fork on the Rancheria Falls Trail, staying close to the reservoir on the wide

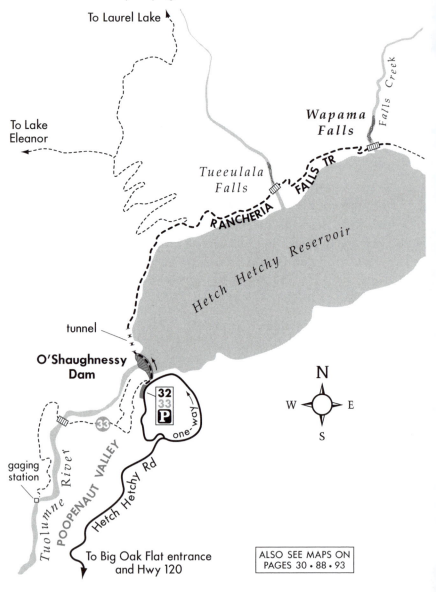

rock shelf. Cross a bridge below seasonal Tueeulala Falls at 1.5 miles, and continue along the talus slopes below the vertical cliffs. Cobblestone steps zigzag down to the base of two-tiered Wapama Falls, where a series of five wood and steel bridges span the boulders over the churning whitewater of Falls Creek. The bridges offer varying views of the foaming rapids beneath your feet. This is the turn-around spot.

To hike farther, the trail contours the cliffs parallel to the reservoir to Rancheria Falls 4.2 miles ahead.

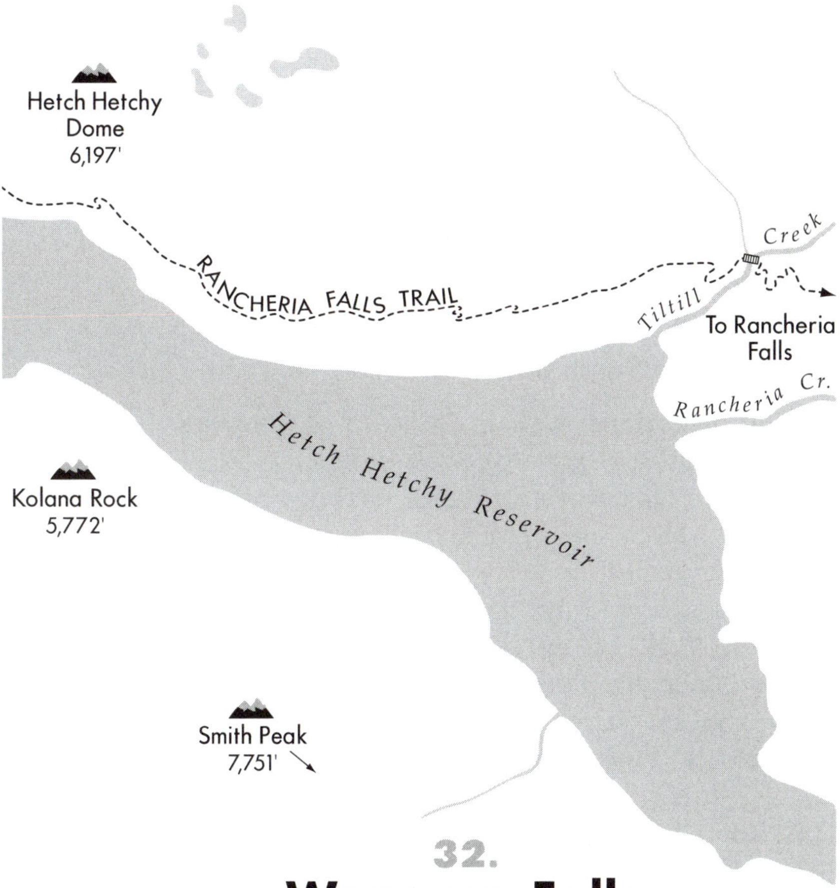

Hetch Hetchy
Dome
6,197'

RANCHERIA FALLS TRAIL

Tiltill

Creek

To Rancheria
Falls

Rancheria Cr.

Kolana Rock
5,772'

Hetch Hetchy Reservoir

Smith Peak
7,751'

32.
Wapama Falls
from O'SHAUGHNESSY DAM
HETCH HETCHY RESERVOIR

33. O'Shaughnessy Dam to Tuolumne River

HETCH HETCHY RESERVOIR

Hiking distance: 2—4 miles round trip
Hiking time: 1—2 hours
Elevation gain: 250 feet
Maps: U.S.G.S. Lake Eleanor

Summary of hike: The O'Shaughnessy Dam rises 312 feet above the Tuolumne River and extends 910 feet between canyon walls at the west end of Hetch Hetchy Valley. The valley is now submerged beneath the Hetch Hetchy Reservoir, which covers 1,861 acres of the narrow, rugged canyon with high granite walls. This hike follows a vehicle-restricted road from the top of O'Shaughnessy Dam to the Tuolumne River at the base of the dam, where a roaring spillway feeds the lower river canyon. The trail continues through the deep granite gorge parallel to the river. Watch for rattlesnakes.

Driving directions: Same as Hike 32.

Hiking directions: Walk downhill to O'Shaughnessy Dam, looking across the clear blue water of Hetch Hetchy Reservoir. Bear left on the paved maintenance road, and pass through the metal gate. Follow the descending road between the rock wall on the left and the narrow canyon and spillway on the right. The pavement soon ends as the road weaves downhill above the Tuolumne River. Just before reaching the tree groves on the canyon floor, the road forks. Take the right fork, heading upstream past lichen-covered boulders to the end of the road in a deep rock gorge at the base of the dam. A column of white-water shoots out of the dam, smashing into the canyon wall. The area may be covered with mist depending on the amount of water being released from the dam. Return to the road fork, and bear right along the valley floor. Cross a bridge over the Tuolumne River in a rock gorge. For a 2-mile round-trip hike, turn around here.

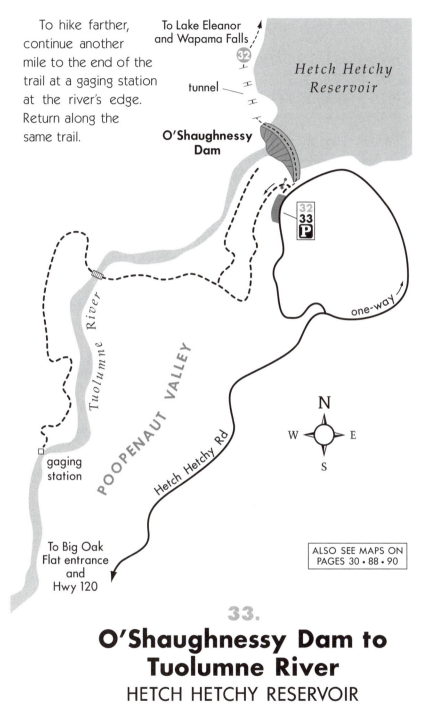

To hike farther, continue another mile to the end of the trail at a gaging station at the river's edge. Return along the same trail.

To Lake Eleanor and Wapama Falls

Hetch Hetchy Reservoir

tunnel

O'Shaughnessy Dam

32
33
P

one-way

Tuolumne River

P O O P E N A U T   V A L L E Y

Hetch Hetchy Rd

gaging station

N

W   E

S

To Big Oak Flat entrance and Hwy 120

ALSO SEE MAPS ON PAGES 30 • 88 • 90

33.
O'Shaughnessy Dam to Tuolumne River
HETCH HETCHY RESERVOIR

34. Poopenaut Valley

Hiking distance: 3 miles round trip
Hiking time: 1.5 hours
Elevation gain: 1,250 feet
Maps: U.S.G.S. Lake Eleanor

Summary of hike: For those who like to have the river all to themselves, this is the hike. Poopenaut Valley, a small, level valley once occupied by cattlemen and sheepherders, sits in the lower canyon of the Tuolumne River downstream from O'Shaughnessy Dam and the Hetch Hetchy Reservoir. The trail to Poopenaut Valley is a brutally steep path, discouraging most hikers. The trail does provide quick and rewarding access to an isolated pastoral area along the Tuolumne River. Watch for rattlesnakes.

Driving directions: From the Big Oak Flat entrance station on Highway 120, drive one mile west (outside the park) to Evergreen Road, the first turnoff on the right. Turn right and continue 7.4 miles to a T-junction at the end of the road. Turn right on Hetch Hetchy Road and drive 1.3 miles to the Hetch Hetchy entrance station. Enter the park and continue 3.9 miles to the posted trail sign on the left. Park in the pullout on the right.

Hiking directions: Cross the road to the signed trailhead, and descend from the Hetch Hetchy Road into the Yosemite Wilderness. The path starts out at a moderately level grade and quickly steepens. Drop into the shady pine, fir, cedar and oak forest, zigzagging down the mountainside. At one mile, the trail reaches a seasonal stream by a waterfall. Curve left and follow the stream to the valley floor. Stroll through the level valley, crossing a large grassy meadow rich with ferns. The path quickly reaches the Tuolumne River at a small beach pocket. Choose your own route up and down the river. At the lower end of the valley are beautiful rock-lined pools. Return along the same trail.

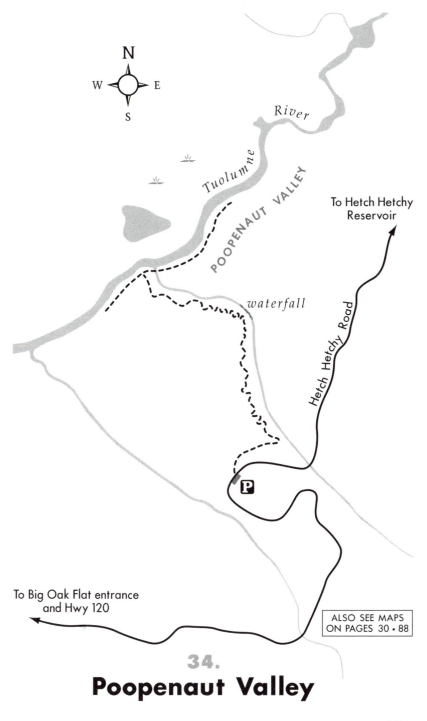

N
W E
S

River

Tuolumne

POOPENAUT VALLEY

To Hetch Hetchy
Reservoir

waterfall

Hetch Hetchy Road

P

To Big Oak Flat entrance
and Hwy 120

ALSO SEE MAPS
ON PAGES 30 • 88

34.
Poopenaut Valley

35. Lookout Point

Hiking distance: 2.7 miles round trip
Hiking time: 1.5 hours
Elevation gain: 500 feet
Maps: U.S.G.S. Lake Eleanor

Summary of hike: Lookout Point is on the crest of a barren granite knoll with panoramic views of the lower Tuolumne River canyon, O'Shaughnessy Dam, and the Hetch Hetchy Reservoir. Atop the 5,309-foot summit are a few scattered Jeffrey pines. The trail begins at the Mather Ranger Station by the Hetch Hetchy entrance to the park. Watch for rattlesnakes.

Driving directions: From the Big Oak Flat entrance station on Highway 120, drive one mile west (outside the park) to Evergreen Road, the first turnoff on the right. Turn right and continue 7.4 miles to a T-junction at the end of the road. Turn right on Hetch Hetchy Road, and drive 1.3 miles to the Hetch Hetchy entrance station. Enter the park and immediately park in the pullout on the right by the Mather Ranger Station.

Hiking directions: The posted trailhead is across the driveway from the Mather Ranger Station. Take the footpath through a small meadow, and enter a forest of ponderosa pine, incense cedar, and black oak to a posted T-junction at 0.2 miles. The right fork leads to Cottonwood Meadow and Smith Peak. Take the left fork and parallel Hetch Hetchy Road, traversing the hillside covered with lupine. After climbing up and over a small rise, curve right, away from the road. Ascend a rocky slope to a plateau between two rocky mountains. In the spring the plateau is lush with streams and wetlands. At one mile is a trail fork with a spur trail to Lookout Point. Bear left, passing a seasonal pond, and curve left. Leave the forest and climb up the smooth glaciated knoll with stunted Jeffrey pines. From the rounded exposed summit are distant views of Tueeulala and Wapama Falls cascading into Hetch Hetchy Reservoir (Hike 32). Return along the same route, or make a loop on the pack trails around the 5,624-foot point.

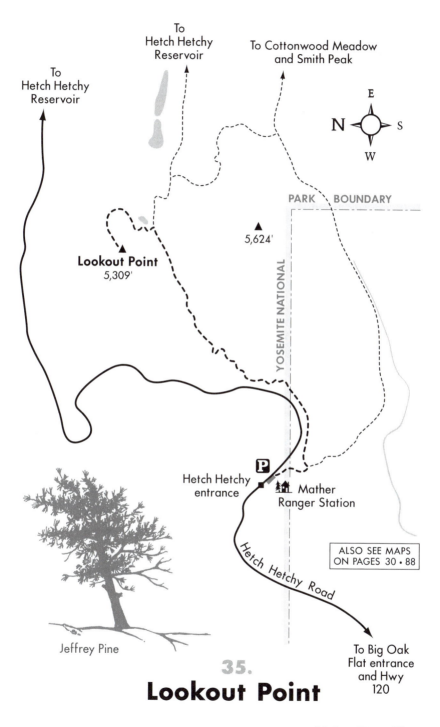

To
Hetch Hetchy
Reservoir

To
Hetch Hetchy
Reservoir

To Cottonwood Meadow
and Smith Peak

N ◇ S
E
W

PARK BOUNDARY

▲
5,624'

Lookout Point
5,309'

YOSEMITE NATIONAL

P
Hetch Hetchy
entrance

Mather
Ranger Station

ALSO SEE MAPS
ON PAGES 30 • 88

Hetch Hetchy Road

Jeffrey Pine

To Big Oak
Flat entrance
and Hwy
120

35.
Lookout Point

36. Carlon Falls

Hiking distance: 3.6 miles round trip
Hiking time: 2 hours
Elevation gain: 200 feet
Maps: U.S.G.S. Ackerson Mountain

Summary of hike: Carlon Falls is a magnificent 35-foot cataract on the South Fork Tuolumne River. The waterfall cascades over wide granite ledges into a large pool surrounded by boulders. The falls was named after Donna Carlon, owner of the Carl Inn Resort from 1916—1938, once located just inside the park boundary. The hike begins in the Stanislaus National Forest on the banks of the river and crosses into the western region of Yosemite National Park. The trail passes the foundation remains of the old resort, following the north side of the river upstream to the pool and waterfall.

Driving directions: From the Big Oak Flat entrance station on Highway 120, drive one mile west (outside the park) to Evergreen Road, the first turnoff on the right. Turn right and continue one mile to the bridge crossing the South Fork Tuolumne River. Park immediately after crossing the bridge in the pullout on the right.

Hiking directions: Take the unsigned path along the north bank of the South Fork Tuolumne River. Head upstream through the lush old-growth forest of oaks, Douglas fir, incense cedars, and sugar pines. Enter the Yosemite National Park boundary at just under 0.2 miles, and cross over some old foundation remains from the Carl Inn Resort 100 yards ahead. The trail is not maintained, but it is distinct and follows an easy grade on a soft mat of pine needles. Cross over a few downfall trees on the undulating path. Pass a sandy beach pocket at a half mile, and continue through an understory of ferns. At 1.6 miles, climb up an eroded hillside to the ridge. Gradually descend on the winding path to the river at a left river bend. Cascades and small waterfalls tumble over large rock slabs. The path soon ends by huge, smooth boulders at Carlon Falls.

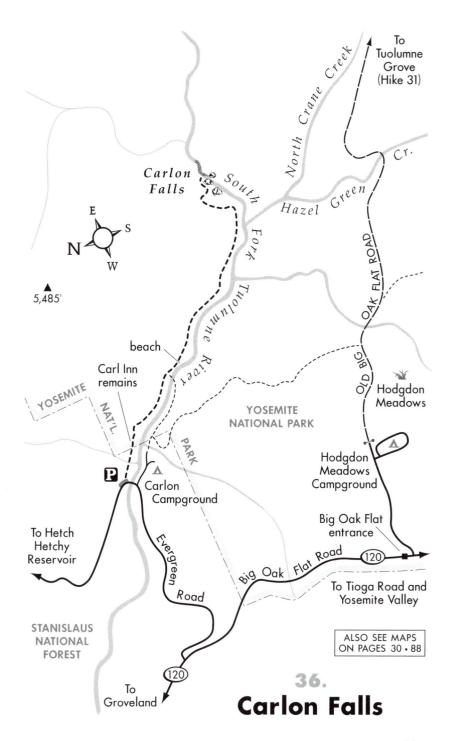

To Tuolumne
Grove
(Hike 31)

North Crane Creek

Cr.

Carlon
Falls

South Fork

Hazel Green

OAK FLAT ROAD

OLD BIG

Tuolumne River

N E S W

5,485'

beach

Carl Inn
remains

YOSEMITE

NAT'L.

PARK

YOSEMITE
NATIONAL PARK

Hodgdon
Meadows

Hodgdon
Meadows
Campground

P

Carlon
Campground

Big Oak Flat
entrance

To Hetch
Hetchy
Reservoir

Evergreen

Road

Big Oak Flat Road

120

To Tioga Road and
Yosemite Valley

STANISLAUS
NATIONAL
FOREST

120

To
Groveland

36.
Carlon Falls

ALSO SEE MAPS
ON PAGES 30 • 88

37. Sugar Pine Grove

Hiking distance: 5.5 miles round trip
Hiking time: 3 hours
Elevation gain: 400 feet
Maps: U.S.G.S. Ackerson Mountain

Summary of hike: Sugar Pine Grove is a magnificent first-growth grove of the largest trees in the pine family. The grove was preserved by a grant from the Rockefeller Foundation and is also referred to as the Rockefeller Grove. The stately sugar pine tree has towering long trunks with diameters up to six feet and enormous cones up to 20 inches long. Sugar Pine Grove resides on the south ridge of North Crane Creek canyon, in the hills two miles west of Tuolumne Grove and three miles north of Merced Grove. The grove rests among a mixed forest with incense cedar, dogwood, black oak, and manzanita. The trail is an abandoned logging road with an easy uphill grade, in use until the early 1940s. With the Merced and Tuolumne giant sequoia groves in the immediate area, most hikers in Yosemite overlook this unsigned trail. The hike offers quiet solitude in gorgeous terrain.

Driving directions: From the Highway 120/140 junction at the west end of Yosemite Valley, take Highway 120 for 13.3 miles to the signed Merced Grove parking lot on the left, located 3.5 miles past the Crane Flat Campground.

From the Tioga Road turnoff, drive 3.7 miles west on Highway 120 to the Merced Grove parking lot on the left.

Hiking directions: Walk 50 yards west down Big Oak Flat Road to the gated dirt road on the right (north). Head north on the gentle uphill grade through a mixed conifer forest. The road is carpeted with a soft layer of pine needles and randomly scattered sugar cones. At 0.6 miles, switchback sharply to the right and continue uphill to the southeast, with a few minor bends in the trail. After curving left, the trail levels out and crosses a broad ridge to the south edge of North Crane Creek Canyon, 1,600 feet above the creek. At 2 miles, curve right and leave the edge of the mountain. Stroll through the level plateau into unmarked Sugar Pine Grove. Surrounded by towering sugar pines, the road ends on a ridge where the only way to continue is down the steep mountain slope. Return along the same trail.

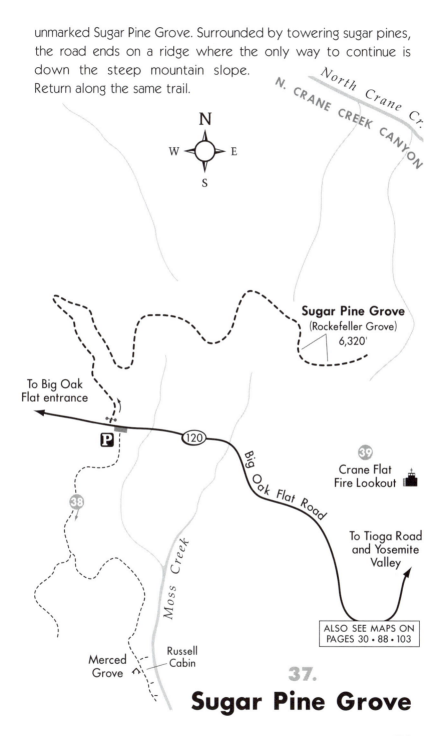

N. CRANE CREEK CANYON
North Crane Cr.

N
W ← → E
S

Sugar Pine Grove
(Rockefeller Grove)
6,320'

To Big Oak
Flat entrance

120

Big Oak Flat Road

P

39
Crane Flat
Fire Lookout

38

To Tioga Road
and Yosemite
Valley

Moss Creek

ALSO SEE MAPS ON
PAGES 30 • 88 • 103

Merced
Grove

Russell
Cabin

37.
Sugar Pine Grove

38. Merced Grove of Giant Sequoias

Hiking distance: 4 miles round trip
Hiking time: 2 hours
Elevation gain: 400 feet
Maps: U.S.G.S. Ackerson Mountain and El Portal

Summary of hike: Yosemite has three giant sequoia groves (Hikes 31, 71 and 72). Merced Grove is the smallest and least visited. It is a dense, natural forest uninterrupted by development. About twenty giant sequoias are scattered within a mixed forest of white fir, incense cedar, ponderosa pine, and sugar pine. The Russell Cabin (also called the Merced Grove Cabin) is an old ranger station that rests in the shady grove. A stream runs through the forest in the canyon. This is not a crowded trail, offering the opportunity to enjoy a quiet and secluded tour of these magnificent trees.

Driving directions: From the Highway 120/140 junction at the west end of Yosemite Valley, take Highway 120 for 13.3 miles to the signed Merced Grove parking lot on the left, located 3.5 miles past the Crane Flat Campground.

From the Tioga Road turnoff, drive 3.7 miles west on Highway 120 to the Merced Grove parking lot on the left.

Hiking directions: From the parking lot, head south through a beautiful forested area along an old gravel fire road. At 0.75 miles is a trail fork. Take the left fork and pass through the gate. For the next mile, descend along the curving road to the canyon floor. At the bottom of the hill, curve to the left. At this curve are six giant sequoias. From here, sequoias are sprinkled throughout the forest. The boarded-up Russell Cabin, built as a retreat for the park superintendent, sits in the grove to the right. Several side trails lead down to the stream and past more giant sequoias. After enjoying the immense trees, return along the same route.

The trail continues along the Old Coulterville Road for 6 miles to Little Nellie Falls, Hike 40.

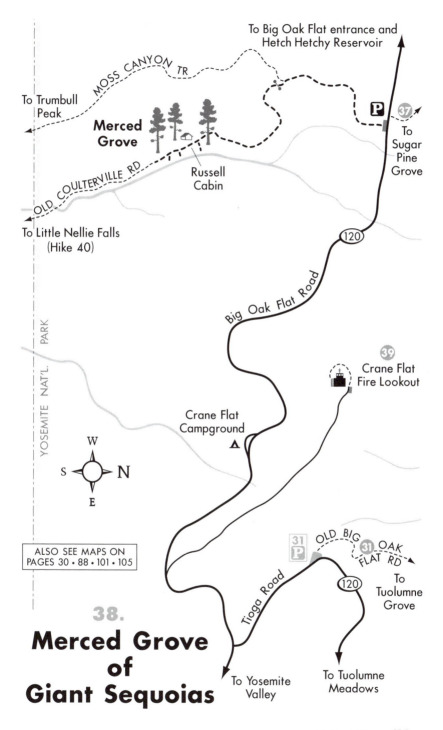

To Big Oak Flat entrance and
Hetchy Hetchy Reservoir

MOSS CANYON TR

To Trumbull
Peak

**Merced
Grove**

P

37

To
Sugar
Pine
Grove

OLD COULTERVILLE RD.

Russell
Cabin

To Little Nellie Falls
(Hike 40)

120

Big Oak Flat Road

YOSEMITE NAT'L. PARK

39

Crane Flat
Fire Lookout

Crane Flat
Campground

W
S — N
E

ALSO SEE MAPS ON
PAGES 30 • 88 • 101 • 105

31
P

OLD BIG OAK
FLAT RD.

31

To
Tuolumne
Grove

120

Tioga Road

38.

**Merced Grove
of
Giant Sequoias**

To Yosemite
Valley

To Tuolumne
Meadows

39. Crane Flat Fire Lookout

Hiking distance: 0.5 miles round trip
Hiking time: 30 minutes
Elevation gain: 30 feet
Maps: U.S.G.S. Ackerson Mountain

Summary of hike: The Crane Flat Fire Lookout lies between Sugar Pine Grove (Hike 37), Merced Grove (Hike 38), and Tuolumne Grove (Hike 31) near the junction of Tioga Road and Big Oak Flat Road. At an elevation of 6,644 feet, the fire lookout offers spectacular 360-degree panoramas of the surrounding mountains in the High Sierras. An interpretive map identifies the names of the peaks within view. This short but phenomenal walk includes vistas to the far distant horizons beyond the park. The lookout is staffed during the summer months to watch for signs of fire. The trail is also used in the winter as a cross-country ski route.

Driving directions: From the Highway 120/140 junction at the west end of Yosemite Valley, take Highway 120 for 9.6 miles to the posted fire lookout road on the right. Turn right and continue 1.4 miles up the narrow, paved road. Park in the spaces on the right, adjacent to the Crane Flat helibase pad.

From the Tioga Road turnoff, drive 0.6 miles west on Highway 120 to the signed fire lookout road on the right. Turn right and follow the directions above.

Hiking directions: Walk down the posted path to the fire lookout, skirting the edge of the helibase pad. Traverse the hillside while overlooking a conifer forest with ponderosa pine, sugar pine, Douglas fir, white fir, and incense cedar. At the Y-fork, bear left, looping counter-clockwise to the lookout tower and the helicopter rescue office. Climb rock and wood steps to the top of the tower for amazing views supplemented with interpretive maps to help identify the peaks.

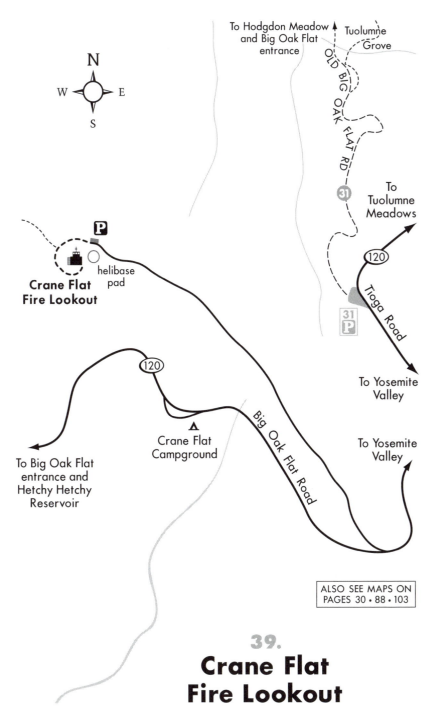

N
W · E
S

To Hodgdon Meadow
and Big Oak Flat
entrance

Tuolumne
Grove

OLD BIG OAK FLAT RD

31

To
Tuolumne
Meadows

120

Tioga Road

31
P

To Yosemite
Valley

P

Crane Flat
Fire Lookout

helibase
pad

120

Crane Flat
Campground

To Big Oak Flat
entrance and
Hetchy Hetchy
Reservoir

Big Oak Flat Road

To Yosemite
Valley

ALSO SEE MAPS ON
PAGES 30 · 88 · 103

39.
Crane Flat
Fire Lookout

Yosemite Valley
MERCED RIVER GORGE to TENAYA CANYON

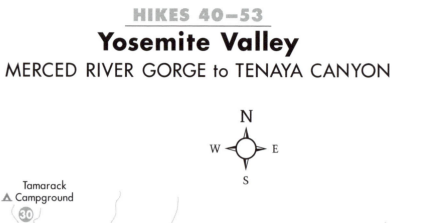

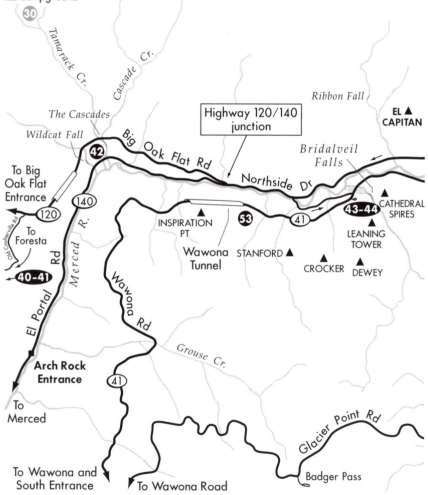

N
W · E
S

Tamarack
▲ Campground
30

Tamarack Cr.

Cascade Cr.

The Cascades

Wildcat Fall

42

Big Oak Flat Rd

Ribbon Fall

EL ▲
CAPITAN

Highway 120/140
junction

*Bridalveil
Falls*

Northside Dr

To Big
Oak Flat
Entrance

140

120

Old Coulterville Rd

To
Foresta

40–41

Merced R.

Merced R.

El Portal Rd

INSPIRATION
PT

Wawona
Tunnel

53

STANFORD ▲

41

43-44

CATHEDRAL
SPIRES ▲

LEANING
TOWER ▲

CROCKER ▲

DEWEY ▲

Wawona Rd

**Arch Rock
Entrance**

41

Grouse Cr.

Glacier Point Rd

To
Merced

To Wawona and
South Entrance

To Wawona Road

Badger Pass

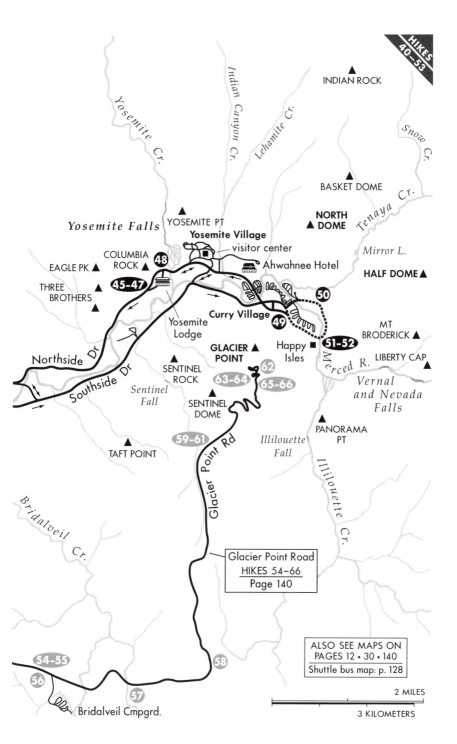

INDIAN ROCK ▲

Indian Canyon Cr.

Lehamite Cr.

Yosemite Cr.

Snow Cr.

BASKET DOME ▲

NORTH ▲ DOME

Tenaya Cr.

Yosemite Falls

YOSEMITE PT ▲

Mirror L.

Yosemite Village

visitor center

COLUMBIA ROCK ▲ **48**

Ahwahnee Hotel

EAGLE PK ▲

HALF DOME ▲

THREE BROTHERS ▲ **45-47**

50

Yosemite Lodge

Curry Village

49

MT BRODERICK ▲

Northside Dr

GLACIER POINT ▲

Happy Isles

51-52

LIBERTY CAP ▲

Southside Dr

SENTINEL ROCK ▲

62

Merced R.

Vernal and Nevada Falls

Sentinel Fall

63-64

65-66

SENTINEL DOME ▲

Glacier Point Rd

Illilouette Fall

PANORAMA PT ▲

59-61

TAFT POINT ▲

Illilouette Cr.

Bridalveil Cr.

Glacier Point Road
HIKES 54-66
Page 140

ALSO SEE MAPS ON
PAGES 12 · 30 · 140
Shuttle bus map: p. 128

54-55

56

58

57

Bridalveil Cmpgrd.

2 MILES

3 KILOMETERS

40. Little Nellie Falls

Hiking distance: 5.6 miles round trip
Hiking time: 3 hours
Elevation gain: 600 feet
Maps: U.S.G.S. El Capitan and El Portal

Summary of hike: Little Nellie Falls is a 30-foot, two-tiered cataract cascading off moss-covered granite into a pool. The trail follows the Old Coulterville Road from Big Meadow to Little Nellie Falls just outside the park boundary in the Stanislaus National Forest. The Old Coulterville Road was the first wagon road into Yosemite Valley. The road dates back to 1874 and once extended 37 miles into the valley. A landslide in 1982 permanently blocked the now abandoned road.

Driving directions: From the Highway 120/140 junction at the west end of Yosemite Valley, take Highway 120 for 3.4 miles to the signed Foresta turnoff. Turn left and continue 1.8 miles on the Old Coulterville Road to a turnout on the right by a forest service information board and a gated road across from Big Meadow. Park in the turnout on the right.

Hiking directions: Walk past the road gate, and follow the Old Coulterville Road past privately owned cabins. Curve around the west end of Big Meadow, and cross an old wooden bridge over Crane Creek. Curve right and head up the hillside on the open terrain to views of El Capitan and Half Dome in Yosemite Valley. At 0.8 miles is an unmarked road fork. Stay to the right and continue uphill. Pass a road gate, and drop into the shade of a conifer forest. At the road split, take the left fork and curve west on the winding road. Cross the hillside above the deep Little Crane Creek valley, with views of Eagle Peak to the south and Buena Vista to the west. Enter a lush woodland of oak, cypress and pine, and wind 200 feet downhill to the park boundary at a trail gate. Cross into Stanislaus National Forest. In a quarter mile, cross Little Crane Creek. Upstream is Little Nellie Falls. Across the creek and downstream is a shady campsite and bench on a flat overlook of the creek.

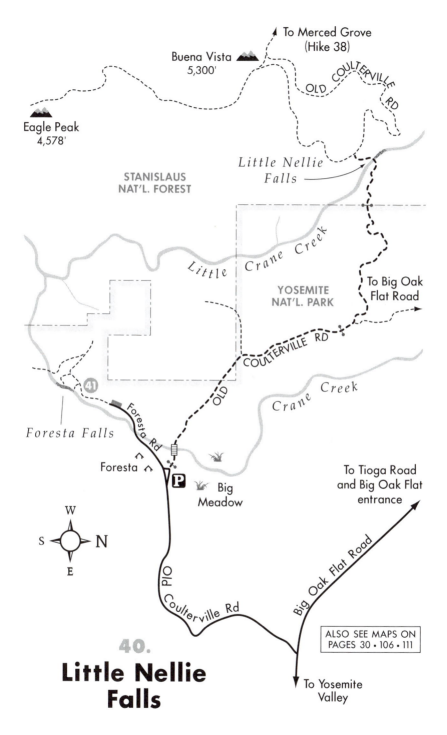

To Merced Grove
(Hike 38)

Buena Vista
5,300'

OLD COULTERVILLE RD

Eagle Peak
4,578'

*Little Nellie
Falls*

STANISLAUS
NAT'L. FOREST

Little   Crane   Creek

YOSEMITE
NAT'L. PARK

To Big Oak
Flat Road

OLD   COULTERVILLE   RD

Crane   Creek

Foresta Rd

Foresta Falls

Foresta

41

P

Big
Meadow

W
S ← N
E

Old Coulterville Rd

To Tioga Road
and Big Oak Flat
entrance

Big Oak Flat Road

ALSO SEE MAPS ON
PAGES 30 • 106 • 111

40.

Little Nellie
Falls

To Yosemite
Valley

41. Foresta Falls

Hiking distance: 1 mile round trip
Hiking time: 30 minutes
Elevation gain: 200 feet
Maps: U.S.G.S. El Portal

Summary of hike: Foresta Falls is a 40-foot waterfall along Crane Creek, a tributary of the Merced River. The tumbling water continues down the creek in a long series of cascades and pools that drop over granite slabs for several hundred feet. The trail begins near the town of Foresta, a small 200-acre settlement tucked into a valley below Big Oak Flat Road. The tiny community, dating back to 1887, is located just inside the park boundary. It was developed as a summer resort in 1887 before it became part of Yosemite National Park. The town had nearly 80 cabins, but the fire of 1990 reduced its size to 17 cabins and a couple of barns. The hike follows an old wagon road built in 1912, connecting Foresta with the town of El Portal at the Merced River.

Driving directions: From the Highway 120/140 junction at the west end of Yosemite Valley, take Highway 120 for 3.4 miles to the signed Foresta turnoff. Turn left and continue 2.4 miles on the Old Coulterville Road to the end of the paved road. Park in the pullout on the right.

Hiking directions: Walk south down unpaved Foresta Road, parallel to Crane Creek. Descend through an open white pine forest in a scorched area from the 1990 fire that burned over 17,000 acres. A side path by five distinct boulders descends to large slab rocks at the creekside. Continue downhill on the main trail. Look back upstream to see Foresta Falls. On the left several faint paths scramble down the hill to the waterfall and various overlooks of the falls. Return by following the same road back.

To extend the hike, the road continues for 5 winding miles, dropping 2,200 feet along the southeast slope of Eagle Peak into the town of El Portal and the Merced River. En route, the road passes two additional waterfalls, one at 1.5 miles and the third at 3 miles.

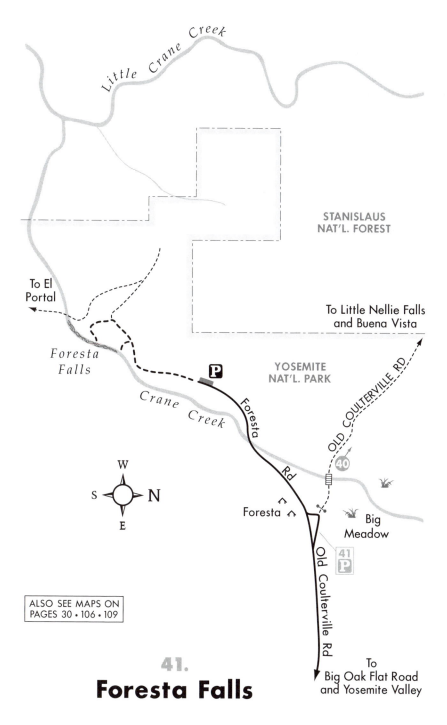

Little Crane Creek

STANISLAUS
NAT'L. FOREST

To El
Portal

To Little Nellie Falls
and Buena Vista

Foresta
Falls

P

YOSEMITE
NAT'L. PARK

OLD COULTERVILLE RD.

Crane Creek

Foresta Rd

40

W
S — N
E

Foresta

Big
Meadow

Old Coulterville Rd

41
P

ALSO SEE MAPS ON
PAGES 30 • 106 • 109

To
Big Oak Flat Road
and Yosemite Valley

41.
Foresta Falls

42. The Cascades and Wildcat Falls

Hiking distance: 0.6 miles round trip
Hiking time: 30 minutes
Elevation gain: 50 feet
Maps: U.S.G.S. El Capitan

Summary of hike: The Cascades and Wildcat Falls reside in the Merced River Gorge two miles west of Yosemite Valley. The Cascades tumble 500 feet down the sloping granite gorge along Cascade Creek to the valley bottom. The frothy whitewater crashes against the granite boulders and empties into the Merced River. Wildcat Falls is a tall, narrow, three-tier waterfall on Wildcat Creek. The cataract freefalls off a sheer granite wall from ledge to ledge, with two 40-foot drops and one 30-foot drop. The lower falls is hidden by tall pines but can be viewed from across the creek. Both waterfalls, separated by a few hundred yards, are dramatically different in size and appearance. Short paths lead to the base of both falls.

Driving directions: From the Highway 120/140 junction at the west end of Yosemite Valley, take Highway 140 (the south fork) for 1.7 miles, following the Merced River to the signed Cascade Falls parking area on the right.

Hiking directions: Begin at the interpretive panels and the overlook of The Cascades. Take the footpath parallel to Cascade Creek. The trail, which includes some boulder scrambling, passes numerous cascades and small waterfalls between the two forks of the creek. After picking your way upstream, return to the parking area.

To go to Wildcat Falls, parallel the road west to Wildcat Creek. Follow the creek upstream through the pine trees to the trail's end at the base of Wildcat Falls. For views of upper Wildcat Falls, return to the road and cross to the west side of the creek.

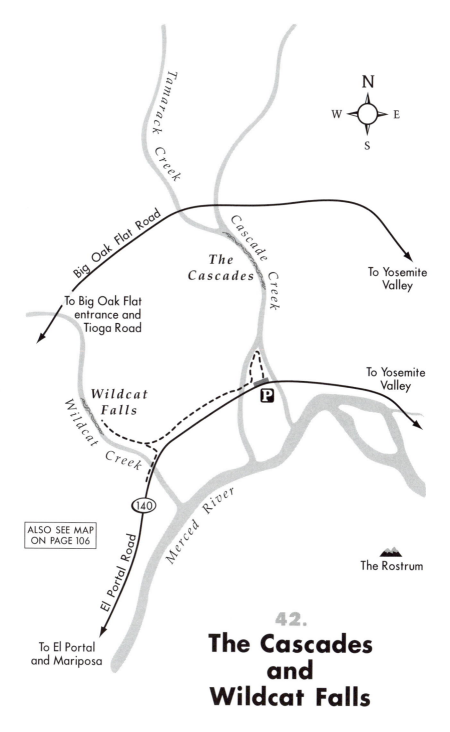

Tamarack Creek

N
W E
S

Big Oak Flat Road

Cascade Creek

The Cascades

To Yosemite Valley

To Big Oak Flat entrance and Tioga Road

To Yosemite Valley

P

Wildcat Falls

Wildcat Creek

To Yosemite Valley

ALSO SEE MAP ON PAGE 106

140

Merced River

The Rostrum

El Portal Road

To El Portal and Mariposa

42.

The Cascades and Wildcat Falls

43. Bridalveil Falls

Hiking distance: 1.2 miles round trip
Hiking time: 45 minutes
Elevation gain: 100 feet
Maps: U.S.G.S. El Capitan

Summary of hike: Bridalveil Falls is a misty, free-falling water-fall resembling a veil when it is blown by the breezes. Its ribbon of water gracefully drops 620 feet off a vertical cliff from the "hanging valley" above to the boulders below on the southern wall of Yosemite Valley. The long fall plunges between Cathedral Rocks and Leaning Tower. This short, one-mile hike leads to Vista Point, a viewing area with a log bench near the base of Bridalveil Falls. The hike continues across three stone bridges over the branches of Bridalveil Creek to a view of the towering El Capitan across the valley floor.

Driving directions: At the west end of Yosemite Valley, the Bridalveil Falls parking lot is located on Wawona Road/Highway 41, just south of the intersection of Highway 41 and Southside Drive.

Hiking directions: The wide, paved hiking trail begins at the east end of the parking lot. Follow the trail about 200 feet to a signed trail fork. Take the trail to the right, leading gently uphill alongside Bridalveil Creek to Vista Point. A boulder field separates Vista Point from the base of the falls.

After viewing the falls from Vista Point, head back to the junction. Instead of returning to the parking lot, continue to the right. Cross the three stone bridges over Bridalveil Creek under a canopy of maple, oak, cedar and bay trees. Curve left to a trail junction a short distance before reaching Southside Drive, the road which loops through the valley. At the trail junction is a picture-perfect view of El Capitan on the north wall of the valley. Return along the same path.

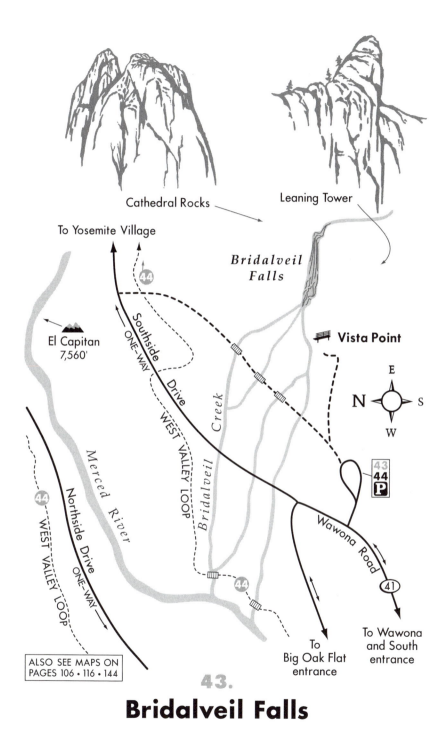

Cathedral Rocks

Leaning Tower

To Yosemite Village

Bridalveil Falls

El Capitan
7,560'

Southside Drive
ONE-WAY

WEST VALLEY LOOP

Creek

Bridalveil

Merced River

Northside Drive
ONE-WAY

WEST VALLEY LOOP

Vista Point

E
N ⬥ S
W

43
44
P

Wawona Road

41

To Big Oak Flat
entrance

To Wawona
and South
entrance

ALSO SEE MAPS ON
PAGES 106 • 116 • 144

43.
Bridalveil Falls

44. West Valley Loop
BRIDALVEIL FALLS to EL CAPITAN BRIDGE

Hiking distance: 6.5-mile loop
Hiking time: 3 hours
Elevation gain: 150 feet
Maps: U.S.G.S. El Capitan and Half Dome

Summary of hike: The West Valley Loop circles the lower end of Yosemite Valley. The hike begins at Bridalveil Falls and heads east as far as Cathedral Beach. The trail skirts the north base of Cathedral Rocks and Cathedral Spires and meanders beneath the 2,600-foot vertical wall of El Capitan. En route, the hike crosses over the Merced River via El Capitan Bridge and Pohono Bridge.

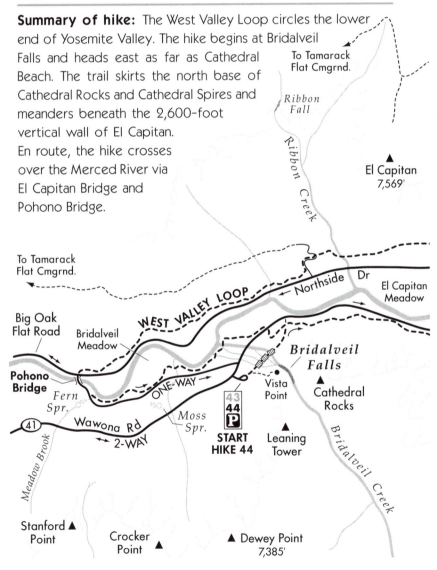

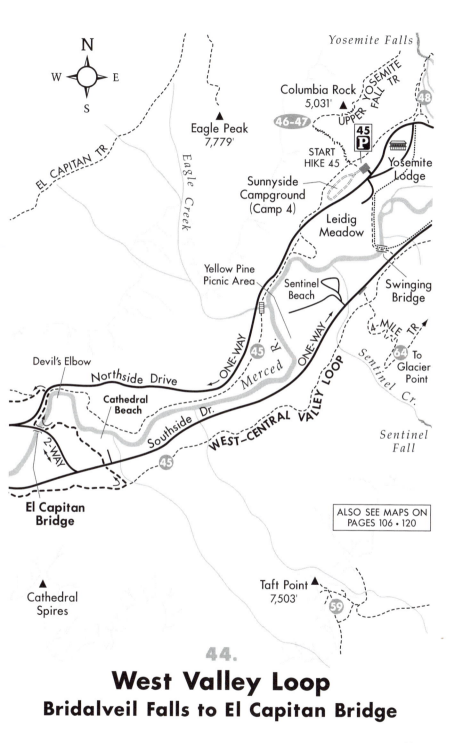

N
W   E
S

Yosemite Falls

Columbia Rock
5,031'

UPPER YOSEMITE FALL TR

46-47

48

Eagle Peak
7,779'

Eagle Creek

START
HIKE 45

45
P

Sunnyside
Campground
(Camp 4)

Yosemite
Lodge

Leidig
Meadow

Yellow Pine
Picnic Area

Sentinel
Beach

Swinging
Bridge

4-MILE TR.

64

To
Glacier
Point

ONE-WAY

45

ONE-WAY

Merced R.

WEST-CENTRAL VALLEY LOOP

Sentinel Cr.

Devil's Elbow

Northside Drive

Cathedral
Beach

2-WAY

Southside Dr.

45

Sentinel Fall

El Capitan
Bridge

ALSO SEE MAPS ON
PAGES 106 • 120

Cathedral
Spires

Taft Point
7,503'

59

44.

West Valley Loop
Bridalveil Falls to El Capitan Bridge

Driving directions: At the west end of Yosemite Valley, the Bridalveil Falls parking lot is located on Wawona Road/Highway 41, just south of the intersection of Highway 41 and Southside Drive.

Hiking directions: From the east end of the parking lot, take the wide, paved trail 200 feet to a signed trail fork. The Vista Point Trail bears right to Bridalveil Falls (Hike 43). Continue straight on the main path, crossing a series of three old rock bridges over braided forks of Bridalveil Creek. At 0.4 miles, just before reaching Southside Drive, curve right on the posted trail, skirting the base of Cathedral Rocks. Traverse the forested, rock-strewn path on the cliffside moraine. Across the river are great views of El Capitan. Slowly descend to the valley floor, tucked into the forest, and walk parallel to the eastbound park road. At 1.9 miles is a signed junction. The right fork leads 4 miles to Curry Village on the West-Central Valley Loop (Hike 45). Bear left and cross the park road by Cathedral Beach. Return northwest, reaching El Capitan Bridge at 2.5 miles. Cross the bridge over the Merced River. Go to the right along the north bank of the river to the U-bend in the river called Devil's Elbow by Northside Drive. Cross the park road and follow the gravel road 50 yards to a footpath on the left. Head west on the posted old road, staying left at a road split beneath 7,569-foot El Capitan, which rises 3,600 feet above the trail. Cross a sandy wash to a T-junction with a gravel road. Bear left 50 yards, then curve right on the trail. Meander along the rolling, forested slopes, passing granite boulders to the park road at Pohono Bridge at 4.8 miles. Cross the road on the historic rock bridge. Bear left and follow the Merced River upstream between the river and Southside Drive. Wind through the forest past Fern Spring, Bridalveil Meadow, and Moss Spring. Cross the road, completing the loop beneath Cathedral Rocks. Return 0.4 miles to the right.

45. West—Central Valley Loop
SUNNYSIDE CAMPGROUND to EL CAPITAN BRIDGE

Hiking distance: 5.5 miles round trip
Hiking time: 3 hours
Elevation gain: Level
Maps: U.S.G.S. Half Dome and El Capitan

*map
next page*

Summary of hike: The West-Central Valley Loop strolls through the middle section of Yosemite Valley adjacent to the West Valley Loop—Hike 44. The hike begins by the Sunnyside Campground, across the road from Yosemite Lodge, and leads into Leidig Meadow alongside the Merced River. The trail makes a loop along the river, weaving through a mixed forest under the base of towering Granite Peak. The Merced River is crossed on both ends of the loop via the El Capitan Bridge and Swinging Bridge. En route, the hike visits Devil's Elbow and Cathedral Beach.

Driving directions: Heading west from Yosemite Valley on one-way Northside Drive, park in the lot on the right, just past Yosemite Lodge and adjacent to Sunnyside Campground (Camp 4). The parking lot entrance is by the road information sign.

Hiking directions: Follow the trail sign to the base of the north canyon wall and a posted trail fork. The Upper Yosemite Fall Trail bears right (Hikes 46 and 47). Take the left fork and walk along the base of the cliffs, passing enormous boulders to Northside Drive. Cross the park road and descend into Leidig Meadow, directly across from Sentinel Rock and Sentinel Fall. Continue south across the open meadow to the Merced River. Twenty yards before reaching the river, take the path to the right and stroll through the meadow to an old, narrow road near Northside Drive. Bear left, following the river's edge, and cross a wooden footbridge over Eagle Creek. Continue through a cedar, pine and oak forest, with views of Three Brothers, El Capitan, and Cathedral Rock. Curve around a U-bend in the river called Devil's Elbow, and continue between the river and the road to El Capitan Bridge beneath the vertical granite monolith. Cross the bridge over the Merced River, and bear left on the posted Bridle Path. Stroll through the forest to the Cathedral Beach entrance road. Thirty yards shy of the road, cross to the south side of the park road and a T-junction. The right fork leads to Bridalveil Falls (Hikes 43 and 44). Bear left and parallel the south canyon wall. Head east to a junction with the Four-Mile Trail (Hike 63). Go to the left to the trailhead at the road. Cross the road and walk through the meadow to the Merced River. Follow the river upstream, and cross Swinging Bridge to the east end of Leidig Meadow. Walk on the paved bike path, parallel to the river. Curve left, leaving the bike path, and walk between maintenance buildings back to the trailhead, directly across the road.

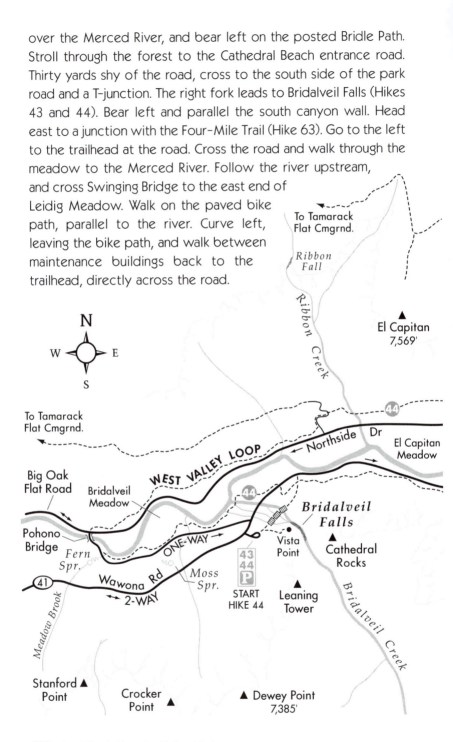

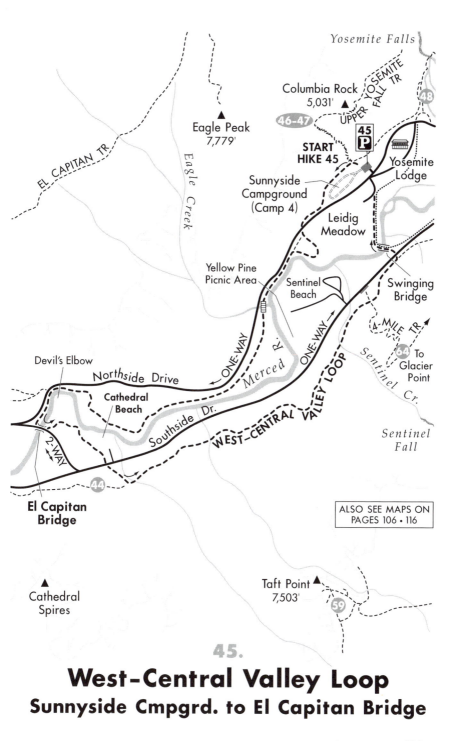

Yosemite Falls

Columbia Rock
5,031'

46-47

UPPER YOSEMITE FALL TR

48

Eagle Peak
7,779'

Eagle Creek

EL CAPITAN TR.

45
P

START
HIKE 45

Sunnyside
Campground
(Camp 4)

Yosemite
Lodge

Leidig
Meadow

Yellow Pine
Picnic Area

Sentinel
Beach

Swinging
Bridge

4-MILE TR.

64

To
Glacier
Point

Devil's Elbow

Northside Drive

Cathedral
Beach

Merced R.

ONE-WAY

ONE-WAY

WEST-CENTRAL VALLEY LOOP

Sentinel Cr.

Sentinel
Fall

Southside Dr.

2-WAY

44

El Capitan
Bridge

ALSO SEE MAPS ON
PAGES 106 • 116

Cathedral
Spires

Taft Point
7,503'

59

45.

West-Central Valley Loop
Sunnyside Cmpgrd. to El Capitan Bridge

46. Upper Yosemite Fall Trail to Columbia Rock

Hiking distance: 2 miles round trip
Hiking time: 1.5 hours
Elevation gain: 1,000 feet
Maps: U.S.G.S. Half Dome

Summary of hike: Columbia Rock is a massive granite rock jutting from the north canyon wall a thousand feet above Yosemite Valley. The rail-lined overlook atop the 5,031-foot rock offers a distinct and detailed view of the valley that includes Half Dome, Sentinel Rock, Cathedral Spires, and far-reaching vistas to the mountain peaks of the Clark Range. This hike follows the first steep mile of the Upper Yosemite Fall Trail—with the aid of 60 switchbacks—through oak and manzanita groves. John Conway and his crew built the trail to Columbia Rock in the 1870s. Hike 47 continues on this trail to the brink of Yosemite Falls.

Driving directions: Heading west from Yosemite Valley on one-way Northside Drive, park in the lot on the right, just past Yosemite Lodge and adjacent to Sunnyside Campground (Camp 4). The parking lot entrance is by the road information sign.

Hiking directions: Follow the Upper Yosemite Fall Trail signs along the east side of the Sunnyside Campground to the posted trailhead. Head up the rock-strewn path, passing huge granite boulders in an oak forest. Begin a steady rhythm of switchbacks on the cliff-hugging trail. At 0.6 miles, the path emerges from the forest directly above Leidig Meadow. Sweeping vistas span across Yosemite Valley. Continue climbing to a trail fork at one mile. The Upper Yosemite Fall Trail continues to the left (Hike 47). Go to the right a short distance to the overlook perched atop Columbia Rock. After savoring the awesome vistas, return along the same route. To extend the hike to the brink of Upper Yosemite Fall, continue with the next hike.

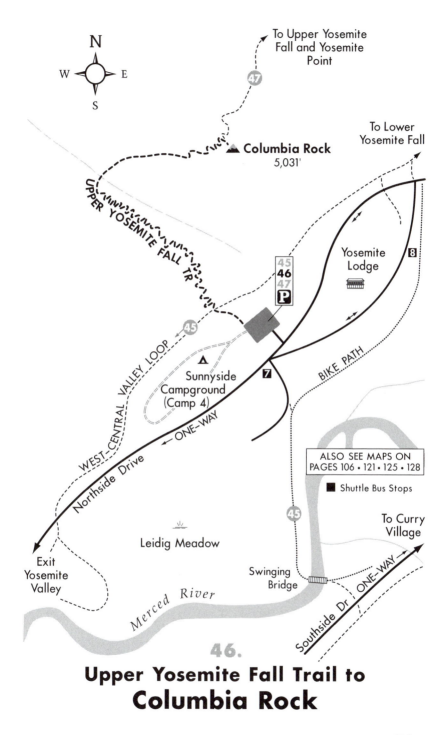

N
W   E
S

To Upper Yosemite
Fall and Yosemite
Point

47

▲ **Columbia Rock**
5,031'

To Lower
Yosemite Fall

UPPER YOSEMITE FALL TR.

45
46
47
P

Yosemite
Lodge

8

45

WEST CENTRAL VALLEY LOOP

△ Sunnyside
Campground
(Camp 4)

7

BIKE PATH

Northside Drive

ONE-WAY

ALSO SEE MAPS ON
PAGES 106 • 121 • 125 • 128
■ Shuttle Bus Stops

45

To Curry
Village

Leidig Meadow

Exit
Yosemite
Valley

Swinging
Bridge

Southside Dr. ONE-WAY

Merced River

46.
Upper Yosemite Fall Trail to
Columbia Rock

47. Upper Yosemite Fall
BRINK of FALLS and YOSEMITE POINT

Hiking distance: 7.2 miles round trip
Hiking time: 6 hours
Elevation gain: 2,700 feet
Maps: U.S.G.S. Half Dome and Yosemite Falls

Summary of hike: Yosemite Falls is the tallest waterfall in North America and fifth highest in the world, dropping 2,425 feet. The Upper Fall plummets 1,430 feet to the middle cascade. The cascade tumbles another 675 feet to the Lower Fall, which plunges 320 feet to the valley floor. The Upper Yosemite Fall Trail is one of the park's oldest trails, built in the 1870s. It is a strenuous and challenging hike—leading from the valley floor and up the sheer north wall to the precipice of Yosemite Falls on the upper plateau. The trail gains 2,700 feet in elevation.

Driving directions: Same as Hike 46.

Hiking directions: Follow the hiking directions of Hike 46 to Columbia Rock. After enjoying the vista overlook at Columbia Rock, continue climbing on the Upper Yosemite Fall Trail. Head up the steep sandy slope and follow a wooded ledge. The trail bends north to the first view of Upper Yosemite Fall. After a short descent, traverse the narrow side canyon with steady close-up views of the falls. Continue up the seemingly endless, tight, steep switchbacks to the plateau atop the valley's north wall, where the trail levels out. Reach a signed junction with the Eagle Peak Trail. Bear to the right (east) towards Yosemite Creek to a short spur trail on the right. The treacherous right fork leads down the cliff face past sculpted rocks and Jeffrey pines. Work your way down granite steps to a railed ledge above Yosemite Creek. The vertiginous overlook teeters over Yosemite Valley from the lip of the falls. Return to the main trail and continue east to Yosemite Creek at a wooden bridge. Cross the bridge and climb 0.8 miles to Yosemite Point for another awesome vista. Return along the same trail.

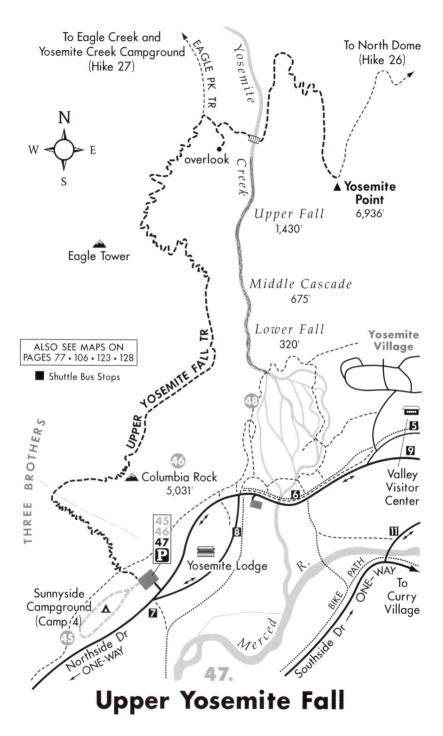

To Eagle Creek and
Yosemite Creek Campground
(Hike 27)

To North Dome
(Hike 26)

EAGLE PK TR

Yosemite

N
W   E
S

overlook

Creek

Eagle Tower

Upper Fall
1,430'

▲ Yosemite
Point
6,936'

Middle Cascade
675'

Lower Fall
320'

Yosemite
Village

ALSO SEE MAPS ON
PAGES 77 · 106 · 123 · 128
■ Shuttle Bus Stops

UPPER YOSEMITE FALL TR

48

THREE BROTHERS

46
Columbia Rock
5,031'

5

9

Valley
Visitor
Center

6

45
46
47
P

8

Yosemite Lodge

11

Sunnyside
Campground
(Camp 4)

7

R.

To
Curry
Village

45

Northside Dr
ONE-WAY

BIKE PATH

ONE-WAY

Southside Dr → ONE-WAY

Merced

47.

Upper Yosemite Fall

48. Lower Yosemite Fall

Hiking distance: 1-mile loop or
     1.5 mile round trip from visitor center
Hiking time: 20 to 45 minutes
Elevation gain: Level
Maps: U.S.G.S. Half Dome and Yosemite Falls

Summary of hike: Yosemite Falls drops 2,425 feet, nearly a half mile, in three tiers from the sheer granite cliff walls. The lower fall plunges 320 feet to a boulder-filled creekbed on the valley floor. This short and busy trail leads to a viewing area at the misty base of the falls at Yosemite Creek. The paved, handicapped-accessible route includes bridges, alcoves, cul-de-sacs, picnic areas, benches, and an amphitheater along the level path. The loop trail weaves through the 52-acre site beneath groves of sweet-smelling pine and incense cedar. Placards highlight the history, geology, and ecology of the area.

Driving directions: Several routes access the Lower Yosemite Fall Trail:
1.) A posted trailhead is directly across Northside Drive from Yosemite Lodge.
2.) A trail leads from the Upper Yosemite Fall Trailhead, adjacent to Sunnyside Campground (Hikes 46 and 47).
3.) Follow the trail signs from Yosemite Village.
4.) Curbside parking spaces are available along Northside Drive, stretching 0.8 miles between Yosemite Village and Yosemite Lodge.

Hiking directions: Several routes access the Lower Yosemite Fall Trail. The trail system and all the routes are well signed. The trail connects Yosemite Village, Yosemite Lodge, and Sunnyside Campground. From Yosemite Lodge, cross Northside Drive to the posted trailhead. From Sunnyside Campground (Camp 4), walk toward the north valley wall to the first junction. The left fork leads to Upper Yosemite Fall (Hikes 46 and 47). The right fork leads to Lower Yosemite Fall. From Yosemite Village, follow the trail signs west.

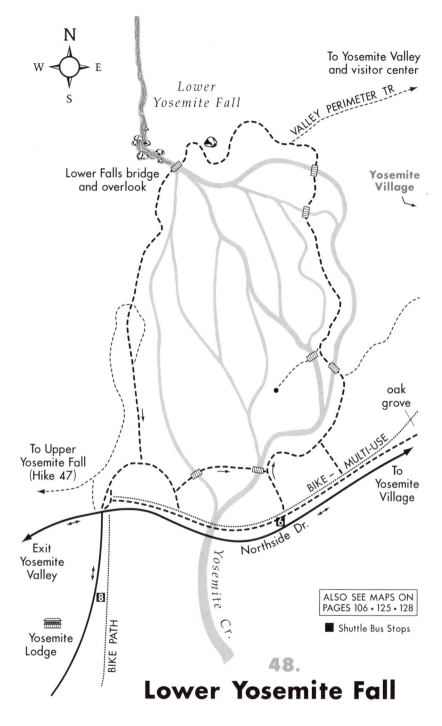

N
W · E
S

Lower Yosemite Fall

To Yosemite Valley and visitor center

VALLEY PERIMETER TR.

Lower Falls bridge and overlook

Yosemite Village

oak grove

To Upper Yosemite Fall (Hike 47)

BIKE – MULTI-USE

To Yosemite Village

Northside Dr.

Exit Yosemite Valley

8

Yosemite Lodge

BIKE PATH

Yosemite Cr.

6

ALSO SEE MAPS ON PAGES 106 · 125 · 128

■ Shuttle Bus Stops

48.

Lower Yosemite Fall

From the trailhead on Northside Drive, between Yosemite Village and Yosemite Lodge, head north on the paved path 50 yards to a low granite stone wall and a junction. The left fork connects to Yosemite Lodge. Stay straight through the conifer forest. Cross a bridge over the stream to another trail fork. Stay to the right toward the vertical north valley wall. Cross a raised wood boardwalk and a bridge to a trail split at 0.4 miles. The right fork follows the Valley Perimeter Trail for 1.2 miles to Yosemite Village and the visitor center. Bear left, looping around a giant boulder to a bridge overlooking the Lower Fall. From the viewing area, the trail loops back to the Upper Yosemite Fall trailhead, Northside Drive, and Yosemite Lodge.

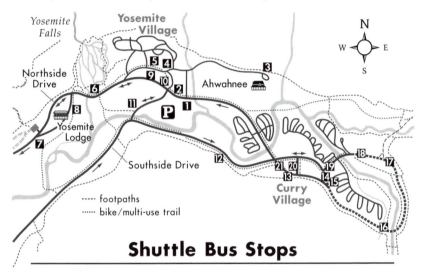

Shuttle Bus Stops

Free shuttle buses run daily 4:00 a.m.–10:00 p.m. Buses stop every 15–30 minutes depending on the time of day and season. Routes and times may change. Check the "Yosemite Today" newspaper for the most up-to-date listings.

1 Yosemite Village: day parking	**11** Sentinel Bridge/Yosemite Chapel
2 Yosemite Village	**12** LeConte Memorial Lodge
3 Ahwahnee Hotel	**13** Curry Village (2 stops)
4 Yosemite Village: Degnan's Complex	**14** Curry Village: parking
5 Valley Visitor Center/	**15** Upper Pines Campground
El Capitan shuttle link	**16** Happy Isles
6 Lower Yosemite Fall	**17** Mirror Lake junction
7 Camp 4: Upper Yosemite Fall trailhead	**18** stables
8 Yosemite Lodge	**19** Lower Pines Campground
9 Valley Visitor Center	**20** Curry Village: parking
10 Yosemite Village	**21** Curry Village: rental center

49. East Valley Loop along the Merced River

Hiking distance: 2.5-mile loop
Hiking time: 1.5 hours
Elevation gain: Level
Maps: U.S.G.S. Half Dome

map
next page

Summary of hike: The East Valley Loop is an easy, beautiful stroll through the far east end of Yosemite Valley. The hike begins at Curry Village and leads through a pine forest to the Happy Isles Nature Center and the tumbling whitewater of the Merced River. The route follows the banks of the river and meanders through meadows with sweeping vistas of the surrounding mountains, including North Dome and Upper Yosemite Fall.

Driving directions: Park in the Curry Village parking lot or take the Yosemite Valley shuttle bus to Stop No. 14 or No. 15. From Curry Village, the trail runs along the south side of the shuttle bus road.

Hiking directions: From the southeast corner of the Curry Village parking lot, take the footpath parallel to the shuttle bus road. Head east towards Happy Isles, passing the tent cabins on your right. Continue one mile through the shady incense and ponderosa pine forest to Happy Isles. Turn right towards the nature center. This is a good opportunity to enjoy the Happy Isles area and the center. To continue with the hike, cross the trail bridge over the Merced River. Take the trail to the left (north), and head downstream along the east bank of the river. (The trail to the right leads to Vernal and Nevada Falls, Hikes 51 and 52.) Continue along the river one mile to the horse stables, with views of North Dome and Upper Yosemite Fall. Cross Clarks Bridge over the Merced River. The footpath soon passes the entrances to Upper and Lower Pines Campgrounds. Turn right at the shuttle bus road, heading towards Stoneman Meadow. Continue back to the Curry Village parking lot on the left.

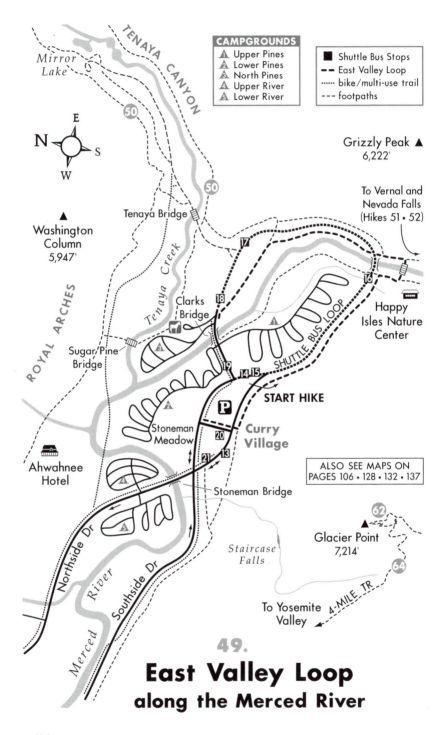

CAMPGROUNDS
- ⛺ Upper Pines
- ⛺ Lower Pines
- ⛺ North Pines
- ⛺ Upper River
- ⛺ Lower River

- ■ Shuttle Bus Stops
- ▬ East Valley Loop
- ⋯ bike/multi-use trail
- --- footpaths

Mirror Lake

TENAYA CANYON

Grizzly Peak ▲
6,222'

To Vernal and
Nevada Falls
(Hikes 51 • 52)

N
E
S
W

Tenaya Bridge

Washington
Column
5,947'

Tenaya Creek

Clarks
Bridge

Happy
Isles Nature
Center

ROYAL ARCHES

Sugar Pine
Bridge

SHUTTLE BUS LOOP

START HIKE

Stoneman
Meadow

Curry
Village

Ahwahnee
Hotel

ALSO SEE MAPS ON
PAGES 106 • 128 • 132 • 137

Stoneman Bridge

Glacier Point
7,214'

Staircase
Falls

Northside Dr

River

Southside Dr

Merced River

To Yosemite
Valley

4-MILE TR

49.
East Valley Loop
along the Merced River

50. Mirror Lake and Tenaya Canyon

Hiking distance: 4.4-mile loop
Hiking time: 2 hours
Elevation gain: 200 feet
Maps: U.S.G.S. Half Dome and Yosemite Falls

map
next page

Summary of hike: Rugged Tenaya Canyon merges with Yosemite Valley and its far northeast end. Half Dome, Washington Column, and North Dome tower over the mouth of the canyon. Tenaya Creek tumbles through the forested canyon for many miles from Tenaya Lake to the Merced River. This hike follows Tenaya Creek up the glaciated drainage, traveling through a cedar, fir and oak forest. The hike includes a visit to vanishing Mirror Lake, which is evolving into Mirror Meadow. The tranquil lake on Tenaya Creek has filled with sediment and become a marshy area with a shallow pool of water and a sand bar beach. From the lake are magnificent views of Mount Watkins, Basket Dome, North Dome, and one of Yosemite's premiere views of Half Dome.

Driving directions: The hike begins from the shuttle bus loop at the east end of Yosemite Valley. Take the free shuttle bus to Mirror Lake/Stop No. 17, or walk to the trailhead, located a quarter mile east of the stables at the end of the valley.

Hiking directions: The hike begins just before the Tenaya Bridge. Instead of crossing the stone bridge, take the footpath to the right, then a quick left. Head upstream along the southeast side of Tenaya Creek. Gently climb past massive, moss-covered boulders to the east shore of Mirror Lake at the base of Half Dome. Continue up canyon along the same side of Tenaya Creek to a bridge at 2.1 miles. From the bridge, the trail loops back along the northwest side of the creek. Continue 0.3 miles to the Snow Creek Trail, which climbs out of Tenaya Canyon to North Dome and Tuolumne Meadows (see map on page 77). Continue walking down canyon. Upon reaching the Mirror Lake meadow, there is an incredible view of Half Dome's 4,700-foot perpendicular face. Mirror Lake used to carry its reflection. From here, take either the footpath or the paved pedestrian road. Both routes will lead back to the trailhead.

The trail is also used by horses, which adds an extra fragrance and several species of flies.

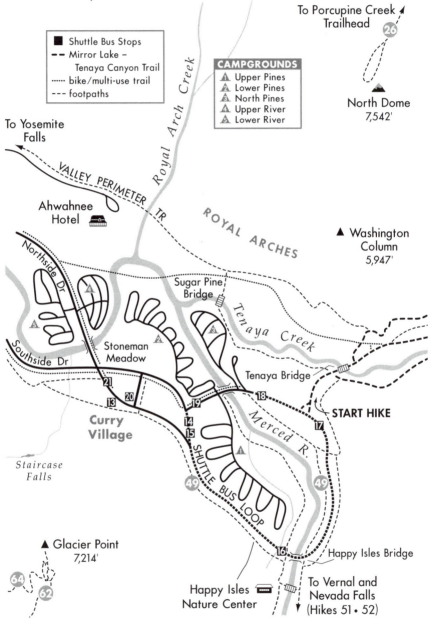

Shuttle Bus Stops
– – Mirror Lake –
     Tenaya Canyon Trail
····· bike/multi-use trail
--- footpaths

CAMPGROUNDS
⛺ Upper Pines
⛺ Lower Pines
⛺ North Pines
⛺ Upper River
⛺ Lower River

To Porcupine Creek ◀
Trailhead 26

North Dome
7,542'

To Yosemite
Falls

Royal Arch Creek

VALLEY PERIMETER TR

Ahwahnee
Hotel

ROYAL ARCHES

▲ Washington
Column
5,947'

Northside Dr

Sugar Pine
Bridge

Tenaya Creek

Southside Dr

Stoneman
Meadow

Tenaya Bridge

START HIKE

21

13 20

19

18

17

**Curry
Village**

14
15

Merced R.

*Staircase
Falls*

SHUTTLE BUS LOOP

49

49

▲ Glacier Point
7,214'

64

62

16 Happy Isles Bridge

Happy Isles
Nature Center

To Vernal and
Nevada Falls
(Hikes 51 • 52)

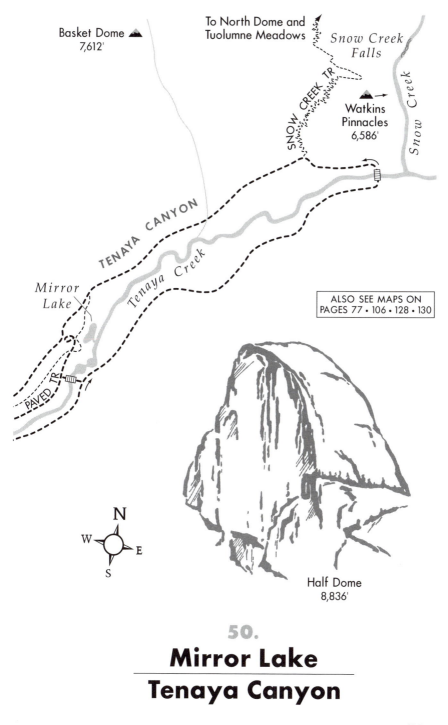

Basket Dome ▲
7,612'

To North Dome and
Tuolumne Meadows

*Snow Creek
Falls*

Snow Creek

SNOW CREEK TR

Watkins
Pinnacles
6,586'

TENAYA CANYON

Tenaya Creek

*Mirror
Lake*

ALSO SEE MAPS ON
PAGES 77 • 106 • 128 • 130

PAVED TR

N
W ✦ E
S

Half Dome
8,836'

50.
Mirror Lake
Tenaya Canyon

Vernal Fall and Nevada Fall

HIKES 51 and 52

Summary of the hikes: At the far east end of Yosemite Valley, the Merced River continues eastward up the craggy Merced River Canyon. Hikes 51 and 52 head up the canyon between Half Dome and Glacier Point among sheer granite walls, deep gorges, and classic glacial features. The trail parallels the Merced River to the base and top of both Vernal Fall and Nevada Fall. These falls are part of Merced Canyon's "Giant Staircase." This glacial stairway plunges 317 feet at Vernal Fall and 594 feet at Nevada Fall. The trail to the falls climbs through the steep granite gorge with stunning views of these two world-class waterfalls. Other awe-inspiring sights along the trail include Glacier Point, Half Dome, Illilouette Fall, and Upper Yosemite Fall. The trailhead is the start of the John Muir Trail, which eventually leads south to the summit of Mount Whitney, 212 miles away.

The hike crosses the Merced River four times via bridges. Along the Mist Trail, moisture from the large volume of water plunging over Vernal Fall coats the canyon walls that have become carpeted with moss, ferns, and deep green foliage. In the spring and early summer, the mist also sprays the trail and hikers. Rain gear is recommended to avoid getting soaked.

CAUTION: Do not swim in the pools above either waterfall. They may look safe and inviting, but they contain strong currents. The consequences of going in could effect the rest of your vacation.

Driving directions for Hikes 51 and 52:

SHUTTLE BUS: From Yosemite Valley, take the free shuttle bus to the Happy Isles Nature Center/Stop No. 16 at the east end of the valley.

ON FOOT: From Curry Village, walk one mile southeast along the footpath parallel to the shuttle bus road to the Happy Isles Nature Center. Reference the map on page 130.

51. Vernal Fall

Hiking distance: 3 miles round trip
Hiking time: 2.5 hours
Elevation gain: 1,000 feet
Maps: U.S.G.S. Half Dome

map next page

Hiking directions: From the Happy Isles Nature Center, cross the bridge over the Merced River. The trail begins on a wide paved path curving up canyon past enormous boulders. The Merced River rages downstream on the right. Across the canyon in a narrow gorge, Illilouette Fall can be seen plunging 370 feet over a vertical cliff from its hanging valley (Hikes 65 and 66). At 0.8 miles, the Vernal Fall Bridge crosses the Merced River. From the bridge is a dramatic view up river of the 80-foot-wide Vernal Fall plunging over the bold granite cliffs. Mount Broderick and the bell-shaped Liberty Cap loom above. Turn around here for a 1.6-mile round-trip hike.

To reach the top of Vernal Fall, continue uphill along the southern bank of the Merced River. A quarter mile past the bridge is a trail fork. The John Muir Trail heads to the right to the top of Nevada Fall—the return trail of Hike 52. Bear left towards Vernal Fall on the Mist Trail, following the canyon's edge. The Mist Trail heads up a series of steep granite steps to the cliff face. Rainbows and billowing mist from the powerful falls levitate in the canyon. Use caution, as the steps can be wet and slippery. At the top of Vernal Fall, large granite slabs and a railing lead down to the brink. Continue following the river upstream a short distance to Silver Apron, a 200-foot cascade sliding over smooth rocks into the green water of Emerald Pool. This is an excellent area to relax and enjoy a rest as a reward for the climb. Swimming in Emerald Pool is discouraged, as it could be very uncomfortable going over Vernal Fall.

To hike to the top of Nevada Fall, continue with the next hike. To return from Vernal Fall, backtrack on the Mist Trail, or make a loop via the Clark Trail up to Clark Point: take the half-mile Clark

Trail up a series of switchbacks to the John Muir Trail. At Clark Point, proceed to the right, heading back to the Mist Trail junction. Cross the Vernal Fall Bridge and return to the nature center.

52. Nevada Fall

Hiking distance: 6 miles round trip (total of Hikes 51—52)
Hiking time: 5 hours
Elevation gain: 1,900 feet
Maps: U.S.G.S. Half Dome

Hiking directions: From the top of Vernal Fall and Silver Apron—where Hike 51 left off—hike upstream to a bridge and cross the Merced River to the north side of the canyon. The trail to the top of Nevada Fall, at the head of the canyon, gains 900 feet in 0.9 miles via switchbacks and granite steps. Near the top, curve along the base of Liberty Cap to a junction. The right fork leads down to the falls. (The left fork leads to Little Yosemite Valley and Half Dome, a popular overnight trip.) At Nevada Fall, just before the bridge, a side trail leads to a spectacular observation platform and railed terrace at the brink of the falls.

The return loop follows the John Muir Trail on the other side of the canyon. Cross the bridge over the Merced River above the waterfall's chute to the south canyon wall. Within minutes is a trail junction. The Panorama Trail to the left leads to Illilouette Fall and Glacier Point, Hikes 65 and 66. Stay to the right, continuing along the John Muir Trail. From the south wall of the Merced Gorge are magnificent views of Half Dome, Mount Broderick, and Liberty Cap towering above Nevada Fall. Continue downhill one mile to another trail junction at Clark Point. The right fork zigzags downhill a half mile and rejoins the Mist Trail just above Vernal Fall. The left fork continues on the John Muir Trail below Panorama Cliff. Both routes join before reaching the Vernal Fall Bridge. Cross the bridge and return 0.8 miles to the nature center.

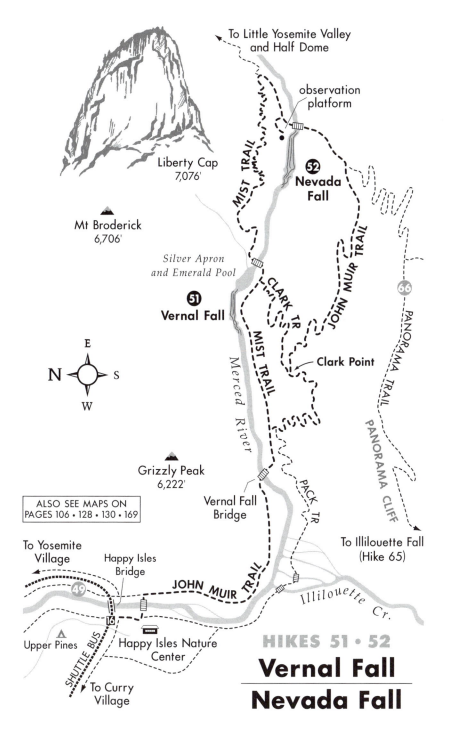

To Little Yosemite Valley
and Half Dome

observation
platform

MIST TRAIL

Liberty Cap
7,076'

52
**Nevada
Fall**

Mt Broderick
6,706'

JOHN MUIR TRAIL

66

Silver Apron
and Emerald Pool

51
Vernal Fall

CLARK TR

MIST TRAIL

Clark Point

PANORAMA TRAIL

Merced River

PANORAMA CLIFF

E

N ✦ S

W

Grizzly Peak
6,222'

PACK TR

ALSO SEE MAPS ON
PAGES 106 • 128 • 130 • 169

Vernal Fall
Bridge

To Illilouette Fall
(Hike 65)

To Yosemite
Village

Happy Isles
Bridge

JOHN MUIR TRAIL

49

Illilouette Cr.

16

SHUTTLE BUS

Upper Pines

Happy Isles Nature
Center

To Curry
Village

HIKES 51 • 52
Vernal Fall
Nevada Fall

53. Inspiration Point
POHONO TRAIL from WAWONA TUNNEL

Hiking distance: 2.6 miles round trip
Hiking time: 1.5 hours
Elevation gain: 1,000 feet
Maps: U.S.G.S. El Capitan

Summary of hike: The Pohono Trail travels along the entire south rim of Yosemite Valley, from the Wawona Tunnel near the valley floor to Glacier Point. This hike begins at the west end of the trail by the Wawona Tunnel and the Discovery View pullouts. The trail climbs a thousand feet to historic Inspiration Point, a rocky promontory at 5,391 feet that overlooks the valley. The hike follows a section of the Old Wawona Road. The road was originally a centuries-old Indian route. The wagon road was built along the route in 1875 and used until the Wawona Tunnel was constructed in 1933.

Driving directions: From the west end of Yosemite Valley, take Wawona Road/Highway 41 for 2.5 miles to the Discovery View parking lots, located just before entering the Wawona Tunnel. Park in the lots on either side of the road.

Heading north on Highway 41, the parking lots are 7.7 miles from the Glacier Point Road turnoff, just after coming out of the Wawona Tunnel.

Hiking directions: From the trailhead sign, immediately begin climbing the south wall of Yosemite Valley. Zigzag up the rocky path and granite slabs while overlooking the magnificent valley and its rock formations and waterfalls. Weave through a forest of black oak, live oak, incense cedar, ponderosa pine, and manzanita. At 0.6 miles, the footpath reaches the Old Wawona Road, an abandoned stagecoach road. The left fork leads two miles to Bridalveil Falls, passing Artist Point en route. Continue straight, climbing through the forest to overlooks of Yosemite Valley and the vertical valley walls on every east switchback. At 1.3 miles, the trail reaches Inspiration Point, with tree-obscured views on a flat bench. Leave the Pohono Trail and head west to the edge of the cliffs. Explore the variety of overlooks on the cliffside terraces.

To extend the hike, the trail continues to Stanford Point, 2.9 miles from Inspiration Point, Crocker Point at 3.4 miles, Dewey Point at 4.2 miles, and terminates at Glacier Point at 11.7 miles.

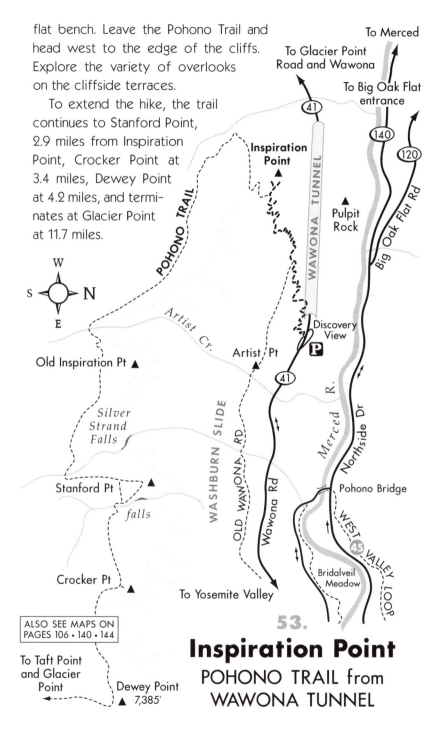

ALSO SEE MAPS ON
PAGES 106 • 140 • 144

53.

Inspiration Point
POHONO TRAIL from
WAWONA TUNNEL

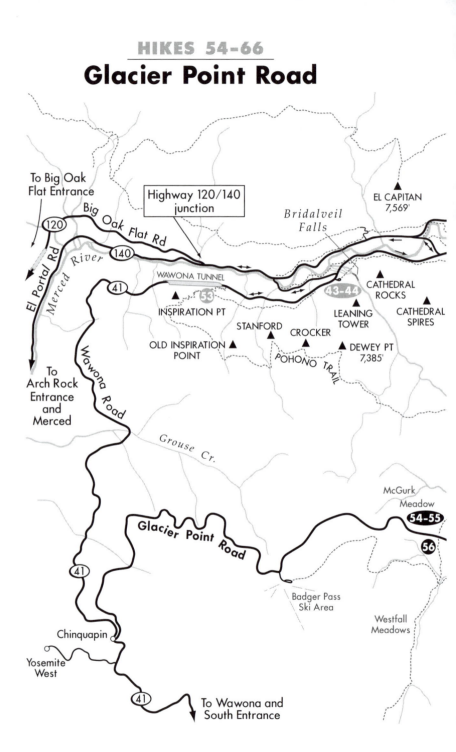

To Big Oak
Flat Entrance

Big Oak Flat Rd

Highway 120/140
junction

El Portal Rd

Merced River

WAWONA TUNNEL

INSPIRATION PT

OLD INSPIRATION
POINT

To
Arch Rock
Entrance
and
Merced

Wawona Road

Grouse Cr.

Glacier Point Road

Chinquapin

Yosemite
West

To Wawona and
South Entrance

Bridalveil
Falls

EL CAPITAN
7,569'

CATHEDRAL
ROCKS

LEANING
TOWER

CATHEDRAL
SPIRES

STANFORD

CROCKER

DEWEY PT
7,385'

POHONO TRAIL

McGurk
Meadow

54-55

56

Badger Pass
Ski Area

Westfall
Meadows

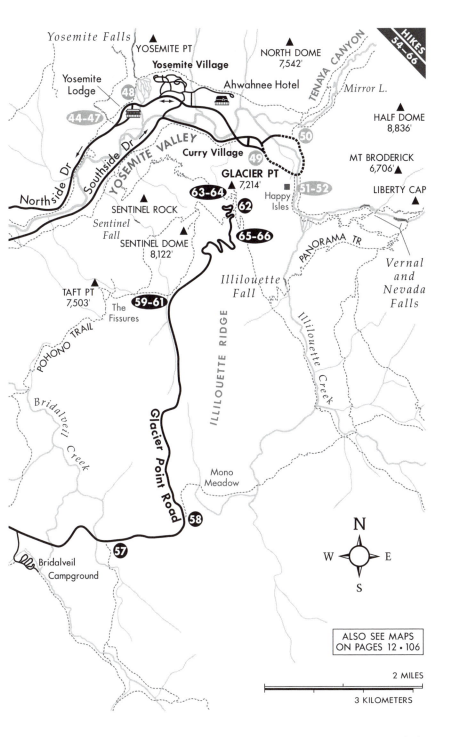

Yosemite Falls

▲ YOSEMITE PT

Yosemite Village

NORTH DOME ▲
7,542'

TENAYA CANYON

Yosemite
Lodge

48

Ahwahnee Hotel

Mirror L.

44–47

HALF DOME ▲
8,836'

Southside Dr

YOSEMITE VALLEY

Northside Dr

Curry Village

49

50

MT BRODERICK ▲
6,706'

LIBERTY CAP ▲

GLACIER PT ▲
7,214'

63–64

62

Happy
Isles ■

51–52

SENTINEL ROCK ▲

*Sentinel
Fall*

SENTINEL DOME ▲
8,122'

65–66

PANORAMA TR

*Vernal
and
Nevada
Falls*

*Illilouette
Fall*

TAFT PT ▲
7,503'

59–61

The
Fissures

ILLILOUETTE RIDGE

Illilouette Creek

POHONO TRAIL

Bridalveil Creek

Glacier Point Road

Mono
Meadow

58

57

Bridalveil
Campground

N
W   E
S

ALSO SEE MAPS
ON PAGES 12 • 106

2 MILES

3 KILOMETERS

54. McGurk Meadow
GLACIER POINT ROAD to POHONO TRAIL

Hiking distance: 3.8 miles round trip
Hiking time: 2 hours
Elevation gain: 200 feet
Maps: U.S.G.S. El Capitan and Half Dome

map
page 145

Summary of hike: McGurk Meadow is a pristine mile-long meadow atop the south plateau of Yosemite Valley. A tributary of Bridalveil Creek meanders through its center. The McGurk Meadow Trail leads downhill through a fir and pine forest to the stream-fed meadow, connecting with the Pohono Trail (Hike 55). At the edge of the meadow is an old pioneer cabin built in the 1890s by John McGurk, who used it as a summer home while grazing sheep.

Driving directions: From the west end of Yosemite Valley, drive 9 miles south on Wawona Road/Highway 41 to Glacier Point Road. Turn left (east) on Glacier Point Road, and continue 7.6 miles to the parking pullout on the left, 70 yards past the signed trailhead on the left. The pullout is 0.1 mile west of the Bridalveil Campground.

Hiking directions: Return 70 yards west on Glacier Point Road to the posted McGurk Meadow Trail on the right. Take the footpath north into the lodgepole pine forest, and walk along the gentle downslope grade. John McGurk's old log cabin is located on the left side of the trail at 0.7 miles. A hundred yards past the cabin, emerge from the forest into McGurk Meadow. Cross a wooden footbridge over the small stream that snakes through the grassy meadow. Skirt the west edge of the meadow, tucked inside the treeline. Reenter the forest beyond McGurk Meadow, and gradually descend to a Y-fork with the Pohono Trail at 1.9 miles. This is the turn-around spot.

To continue hiking, the Pohono Trail travels along the south rim of Yosemite Valley for 13 miles, from Glacier Point at the east end to Inspiration Point and the Wawona Tunnel at the west end. En route to Inspiration Point is Dewey Point and Crocker Point—Hike 55.

55. Dewey Point and Crocker Point
POHONO TRAIL (West End)

Hiking distance: 7.8—9.2 miles round trip
Hiking time: 4 hours
Elevation gain: 400 feet
Maps: U.S.G.S. El Capitan and Half Dome

map
next page

Summary of hike: This hike weaves through McGurk Meadow to the towering south rim of Yosemite Valley en route to Dewey Point and Crocker Point. The two overlooks are perched 3,500 feet and 3,100 feet above the valley floor. From the overlooks are sweeping bird's-eye views of the entire valley, from Tenaya Canyon to El Capitan. The incredible views include Half Dome, Clouds Rest, Cathedral Rocks, Cathedral Spires, Leaning Tower, Bridalveil Fall, Yosemite Falls, Three Brothers, and Mount Hoffman.

Driving directions: Same as Hike 54.

Hiking directions: Take the McGurk Meadow Trail to the Pohono Trail junction, following the hiking directions for Hike 54. To the right, the Pohono Trail leads to Taft Point and Glacier Point (Hikes 59 and 62). Take the Pohono Trail to the left and head west through the forest. Cross a tributary stream of Bridalveil Creek and ascend a hill, crossing a second feeder stream. Steadily climb through an old growth forest to a clearing near the ridge where the trail levels out. The views open to the Merced River Canyon beyond Glacier Point and across Yosemite Valley to the north rim. The path reaches Dewey Point by a deep cleft. To the right, a path leads out on the rock shelf point.

To continue to Crocker Point, bear left and follow the edge of the 3,000-foot cliffs, marveling at the staggering views. Climb the hill through a pine grove, back from the cliff's edge. Descend to Crocker Point on a rocky flat that extends out on an over-hanging cliff. This is the turn-around point.

To hike farther, the Pohono Trail continues to Stanford Point, 0.5 miles ahead; Inspiration Point, 3.4 miles ahead; and down to the valley floor at the Wawona Tunnel, 4.7 miles ahead. (See Hike 53.)

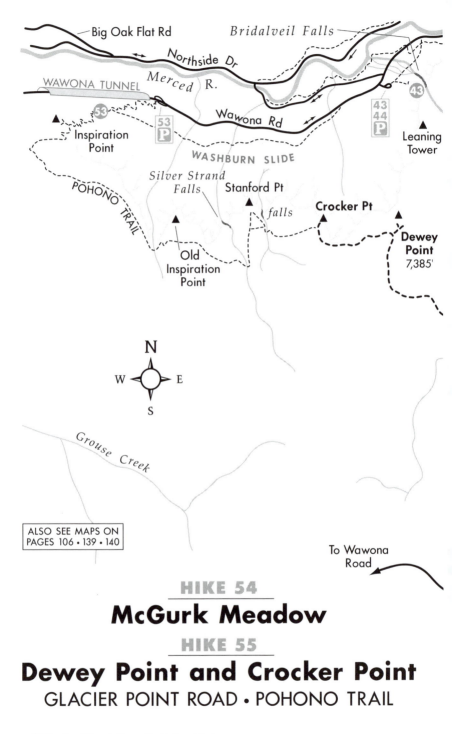

HIKE 54
McGurk Meadow
HIKE 55
Dewey Point and Crocker Point
GLACIER POINT ROAD • POHONO TRAIL

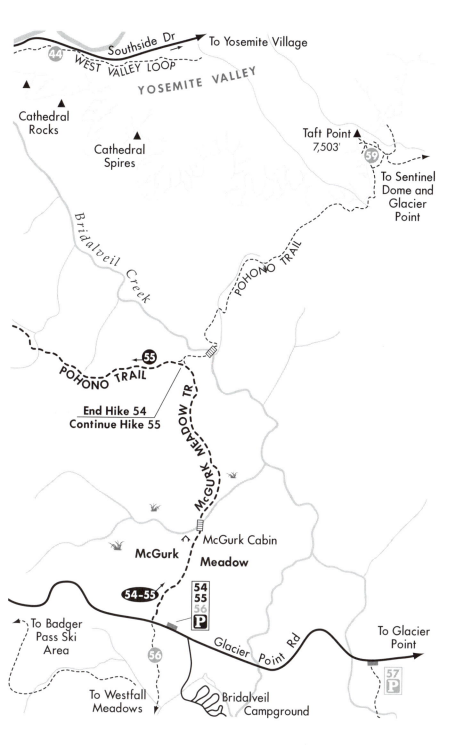

To Yosemite Village

Southside Dr

WEST VALLEY LOOP 44

YOSEMITE VALLEY

Cathedral Rocks

Cathedral Spires

Taft Point
7,503'

59

To Sentinel Dome and Glacier Point

Bridalveil Creek

POHONO TRAIL

POHONO TRAIL 55

**End Hike 54
Continue Hike 55**

McGURK MEADOW TR

McGurk Cabin

McGurk Meadow

54-55

54 55 56 P

To Badger Pass Ski Area

56

To Westfall Meadows

Glacier Point Rd

To Glacier Point

57 P

Bridalveil Campground

56. Westfall Meadows

Hiking distance: 3.4 miles round trip
Hiking time: 1.5 hours
Elevation gain: 200 feet
Maps: U.S.G.S. El Capitan

Summary of hike: The Westfall Meadows Trail connects Glacier Point Road to Wawona. The trail leads through Westfall Meadows, a half-mile-long meadow surrounded by pines. The path follows a gentle grade through the forest, away from Yosemite's summer crowds. The meadow, a short distance from Bridalveil Campground, can be wet during the spring and early summer. The stream draining the meadow flows through the campground before merging with Bridalveil Creek.

Driving directions: Same as Hike 54. The Westfall Meadows Trail is directly across the road from the McGurk Meadow Trail.

Hiking directions: Return 70 yards west on Glacier Point Road to the posted McGurk Meadow Trail on the right. Cross the road to the unsigned but distinct trail on the left, across from the McGurk Meadow Trail. Head south into the Yosemite Wilderness at a trail sign. Follow the level path through an open pine forest, and gradually descend across large granite slabs and boulders. Cross a tributary stream of Bridalveil Creek. Parallel the stream, skirting the west side of a meadow to an old road crossing the trail. To the left, the road leads to Bridalveil Campground; to the right it leads to Badger Pass Ski Area. Continue south on the footpath, winding through the forest above the drainage stream from Westfall Meadows. Emerge from the forest at Westfall Meadows, a large grassy meadow rimmed with pines. The open expanse is marbled with waterways. Early in the season, the meadow is marshy. A faint path crosses through the center of the meadow to the hills in the south. This is the turn-around spot.

To hike farther, the trail continues to Deer Camp 3.5 miles ahead and Wawona, 11.5 miles ahead. En route the trail follows Alder Creek to Alder Falls.

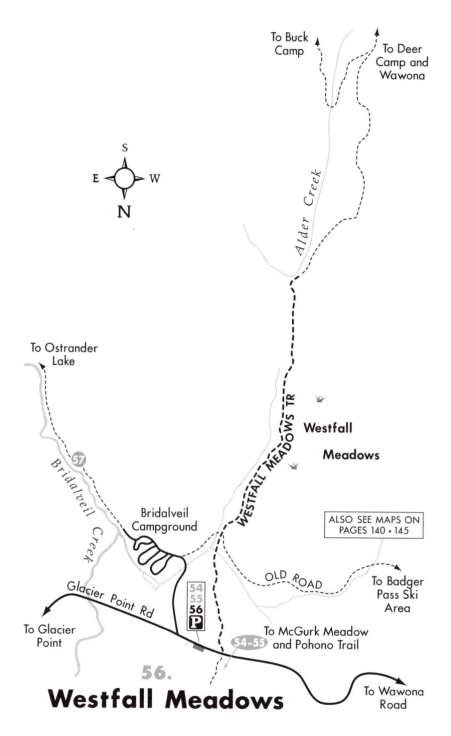

To Buck
Camp

To Deer
Camp and
Wawona

S
E ⊕ W
N

Alder Creek

To Ostrander
Lake

WESTFALL MEADOWS TR

Westfall

Meadows

57

Bridalveil Creek

Bridalveil
Campground

ALSO SEE MAPS ON
PAGES 140 · 145

OLD ROAD

To Badger
Pass Ski
Area

Glacier Point Rd

54
55
56
P

To Glacier
Point

54 55

To McGurk Meadow
and Pohono Trail

56.
Westfall Meadows

To Wawona
Road

57. Bridalveil Creek

Hiking distance: 5.5—7 miles round trip
Hiking time: 3 hours
Elevation gain: Near level
Maps: U.S.G.S. Half Dome

Summary of hike: The headwaters of Bridalveil Creek begin at Ostrander Lake at an elevation of 8,505 feet. After flowing across the high plateau, the creek drops 620 feet over the south wall of Yosemite Valley before joining the Merced River (Hike 43). This level trail parallels Bridalveil Creek atop the plateau through lodgepole pine forests and meadows. It is a quiet, away-from-the-crowds hike. Wildflowers are abundant along the meadows and the two creek crossings. The trail is also a popular cross-country ski trail during the winter that leads to a hut at Ostrander Lake. A few miles downstream from this hike, the creek drops over Bridalveil Falls.

Driving directions: From the west end of Yosemite Valley, drive 9 miles south on Wawona Road/Highway 41 to Glacier Point Road. Turn left (east) on Glacier Point Road, and continue 9.1 miles to the Ostrander Lake Trail parking pullout on the right. The posted pullout is 1.3 miles past the Bridalveil Campground.

Hiking directions: From the Ostrander Lake Trailhead, walk south through the lodgepole pine forest on level terrain. At 0.2 miles, a wooden footbridge crosses a tributary of Bridalveil Creek. Continue 1.4 miles through the regenerating forest and meadow to a trail junction. The left fork heads to Ostrander Lake, 4.5 miles ahead. Take the right fork leading to the Bridalveil Creek Campground. Descend and cross Bridalveil Creek in less than a quarter mile, using boulders as stepping stones. A short distance past the creek is another junction. The left fork leads to Wawona. Again, take the right fork. Parallel Bridalveil Creek to the camp-ground, 1.7 miles from the junction. To return, follow the same trail back, or walk 1.3 miles east on Glacier Point Road.

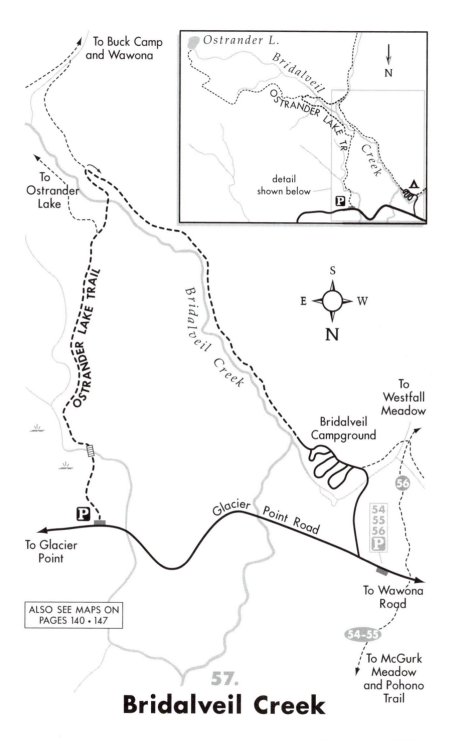

To Buck Camp
and Wawona

Ostrander L.

Bridalveil

OSTRANDER LAKE TR

Creek

detail
shown below

P

To
Ostrander
Lake

OSTRANDER LAKE TRAIL

Bridalveil Creek

S

E — W

N

Bridalveil
Campground

To
Westfall
Meadow

56

P

Glacier Point Road

54
55
56
P

To Glacier
Point

To Wawona
Road

ALSO SEE MAPS ON
PAGES 140 · 147

54-55

To McGurk
Meadow
and Pohono
Trail

57.

Bridalveil Creek

58. Mono Meadow to overlook

Hiking distance: 3.5 miles round trip
Hiking time: 2 hours
Elevation gain: 400 feet
Maps: U.S.G.S. Half Dome

Summary of hike: Mono Meadow is a perpetually wet, marshy meadow fringed with lodgepole pines. The first half mile of the trail steeply descends into the meadow. Downfall logs are used to cross the meandering streams and meadow bogs as you make your way across the meadow. The trail crosses a major tributary of Illilouette Creek and leads to a ridge with a vista point of Mount Starr King, a prominent 9,092-foot dome in the Clark Range. From the granite knoll overlook are views of North Dome, Basket Dome, Half Dome, and Clouds Rest.

Driving directions: From the west end of Yosemite Valley, drive 9 miles south on Wawona Road/Highway 41 to Glacier Point Road. Turn left (east) on Glacier Point Road, and continue 10.3 miles to the posted parking area on the right.

Hiking directions: Take the signed trail north, and traverse the east-facing slope past a grove of mature red fir. Descend 250 feet through the forest in less than a half mile. From here, the rest of the hike is fairly level. Cross a tributary stream of Illilouette Creek and meander into Mono Meadow, a small, undisturbed meadow. A stream flows through the flat meadow, making the area swampy. Cross through the marshy parts of the meadow on downfall logs. After crossing, pick up the dry trail on the east end of the meadow. Continue through the shady red and white fir forest on a low divide to a fork of Illilouette Creek, tumbling through a rocky gorge with cascades and waterfalls. Carefully cross logs over the creek, and wind through the nearly flat forest. A half mile beyond the creek is an unmarked clearing on a knoll, just before the trail steeply descends. Leave the trail to the left, and cross the clearing to the plainly visible polished granite slab for the best panoramas. This is the turn-around spot.

To hike farther, the trail descends from the overlook and connects with the Panorama Trail above Illilouette Fall, 4 miles ahead (Hike 65).

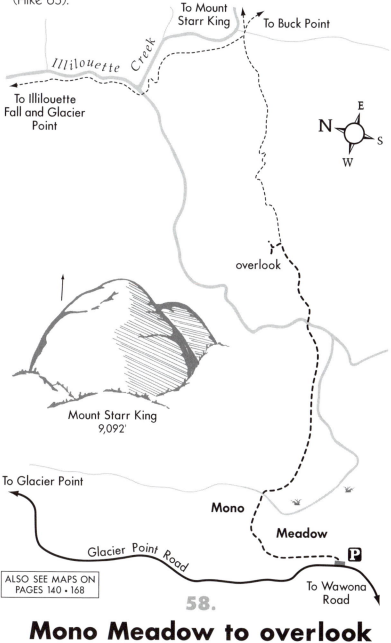

To Mount Starr King

To Buck Point

Illilouette Creek

To Illilouette Fall and Glacier Point

N E S W

overlook

Mount Starr King
9,092'

To Glacier Point

Mono

Meadow

P

Glacier Point Road

To Wawona Road

ALSO SEE MAPS ON
PAGES 140 • 168

58.

Mono Meadow to overlook

59. Taft Point and The Fissures

Hiking distance: 2.2 miles round trip
Hiking time: 1.5 hours
Elevation gain: 250 feet
Maps: U.S.G.S. Half Dome

Summary of hike: Taft Point is a rocky knoll that overhangs the south rim of Yosemite Valley 3,500 feet above the valley floor (cover photo). The Fissures on Profile Cliff are five vertical fractures in the overhanging cliff, creating crevasses in the huge granite masses hundreds of feet deep. These deep and narrow chasms and Taft Point are absolutely stunning. This area has truly spectacular views of Yosemite Valley, including El Capitan, Three Brothers, and Yosemite Falls.

Driving directions: From the west end of Yosemite Valley, drive 9 miles south on Wawona Road/Highway 41 to Glacier Point Road. Turn left (east) on Glacier Point Road, and continue 13.4 miles to the trailhead parking lot on the left side of the road.

Hiking directions: From the parking lot, head northwest to a trail junction 150 feet ahead. To the right is Sentinel Dome, Hike 60. Take the trail to the left. Taft Point is 1.1 mile ahead. A short distance from the junction is a beautiful white quartz outcropping. Descend and cross Sentinel Creek, the source of Sentinel Fall. Continue through an evergreen forest to a junction 0.6 miles from the trailhead. The Pohono Trail to the right leads to Sentinel Dome and Glacier Point (Hike 61). Take the left trail through a shady, lush meadow. Weave through the forest past large boulders. Descend to a grand vista of Yosemite Valley, and walk down rock steps to The Fissures. There are no railings—use *extreme caution.* After peering down The Fissures and the 3,000-foot ledge, climb up the angular rock to the railing at the tip of Taft Point. From this open, elevated perch, choose your own route. This is an amazing and unique area to explore. Return along the same trail.

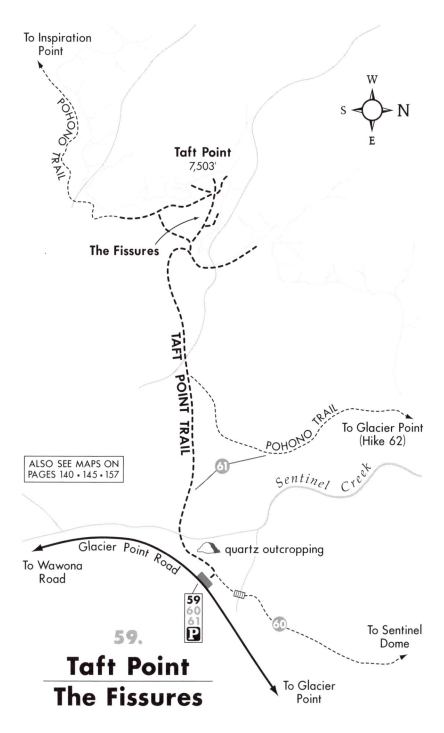

To Inspiration Point

POHONO TRAIL

W
S ✕ N
E

Taft Point
7,503'

The Fissures

TAFT POINT TRAIL

ALSO SEE MAPS ON
PAGES 140 • 145 • 157

POHONO TRAIL

To Glacier Point
(Hike 62)

61

Sentinel Creek

Glacier Point Road

quartz outcropping

To Wawona
Road

59
60
61
P

60

To Sentinel
Dome

59.

Taft Point
The Fissures

To Glacier
Point

60. Sentinel Dome

Hiking distance: 2.4 miles round trip
Hiking time: 1.5 hours
Elevation gain: 400 feet
Maps: U.S.G.S. Half Dome

Summary of hike: This hike crosses the tree-dotted plateau from Glacier Point Road to Sentinel Dome. The dome offers one of the highest views of Yosemite Valley, second only to Half Dome. Sitting at 8,122 feet and 4,000 feet above the valley floor, Sentinel Dome has sweeping 360-degree views that include Nevada Fall, Liberty Cap, Half Dome, Clouds Rest, Cathedral Rocks, Yosemite Falls, El Capitan, and the surrounding mountain ranges. The unobstructed views are breathtaking in every direction.

Driving directions: From the west end of Yosemite Valley, drive 9 miles south on Wawona Road/Highway 41 to Glacier Point Road. Turn left (east) on Glacier Point Road, and continue 13.4 miles to the trailhead parking lot on the left side of the road.

Hiking directions: From the parking lot, head northwest to a trail junction 150 feet ahead. Take the trail to the right towards Sentinel Dome. (The trail to the left makes a loop to Taft Point, Hike 61.) Cross a stream on a footbridge. Follow the wide sandy path uphill through open stands of evergreens and granite slabs as Sentinel Dome dances in and out of view. As you approach the south base of Sentinel Dome, cairns (manmade rock mounds) mark the route across the open granite. The trail merges with an old, abandoned asphalt road. Follow the road around the east side of the dome to the northern flank. This side overlooks Yosemite Valley and has the least demanding slope to the dome top. (The trail to the right leads to the Pohono Trail.) Turn left and climb up the granite slope, choosing your own route to the summit. Explore the perimeter of the dome for the ever-changing views from the peaks to the valleys. Return along the same route.

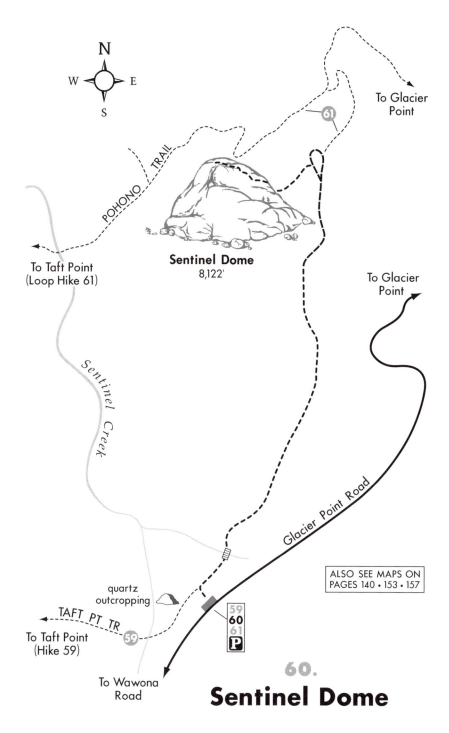

N
W   E
S

To Glacier
Point

POHONO TRAIL

61

To Taft Point
(Loop Hike 61)

Sentinel Dome
8,122'

To Glacier
Point

Sentinel Creek

Glacier Point Road

ALSO SEE MAPS ON
PAGES 140 • 153 • 157

quartz
outcropping

TAFT PT TR

59

To Taft Point
(Hike 59)

59
60
61
P

To Wawona
Road

60.
Sentinel Dome

61. Pohono Trail Loop
TAFT POINT to SENTINEL DOME

Hiking distance: 4.3-mile loop plus 1 mile to explore Taft
Point and Sentinel Dome
Hiking time: 2—3 hours
Elevation gain: 500 feet
Maps: U.S.G.S. Half Dome

Summary of hike: The Pohono Trail is a 13-mile trail atop
Yosemite Valley's south rim. This loop on the trail's east side leads
to Taft Point (Hike 59) and circles around Sentinel Dome (Hike
60). From the 3,000-foot cliffs, the loop includes some of the
best views of Yosemite Valley and the surrounding rock formations. Highlights include panoramic vistas of Yosemite Falls, El
Capitan, and leg-weakening views down to the valley bottom.
The Pohono Trail connects Glacier Point at the east end of Glacier
Point Road (Hike 62) to Inspiration Point and the Wawona Tunnel
at the west end of Yosemite Valley (Hike 53).

Driving directions: From the west end of Yosemite Valley,
drive 9 miles south on Wawona Road/Highway 41 to Glacier
Point Road. Turn left (east) on Glacier Point Road, and continue
13.4 miles to the signed parking area on the left side of the road.

Hiking directions: Take the trail west (left) towards Taft
Point. Walk through an open pine forest, and pass a huge quartz
outcropping. Boulder-hop over Sentinel Creek to a posted junction at 0.6 miles. Straight ahead to the west is The Fissures and
Taft Point. Reference Hike 59 to explore the spectacular point.
Return and take the Pohono Trail to the north towards Sentinel
Dome. Descend through Jeffrey pine and red fir, following the
pathway between large boulder outcroppings. Walk through the
bucolic forest and through another garden of boulders to the
edge of the 3,000-foot cliffs. Follow the cliff's edge past magnificent rock formations and vistas. Cross Sentinel Creek to a
junction. The left fork is a short detour to an overlook of
Yosemite Valley at the edge of the cliffs. Continue on the main

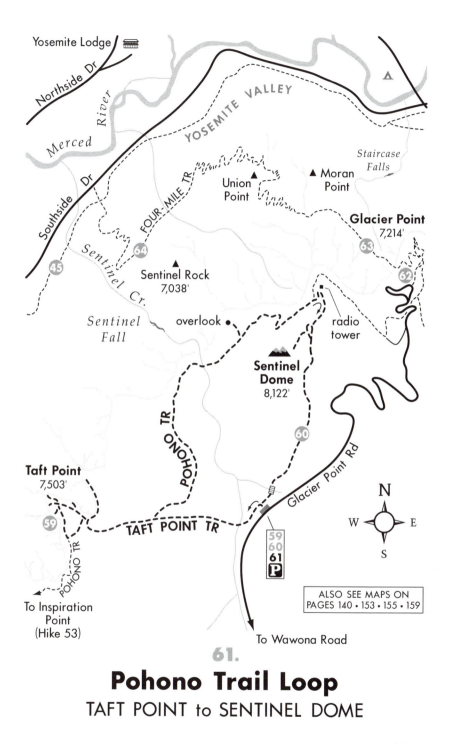

Yosemite Lodge

Northside Dr

Merced River

Southside Dr

YOSEMITE VALLEY

Staircase Falls

FOUR-MILE TR

Union Point

▲ Moran Point

Glacier Point
7,214'

Sentinel Cr.

64

45

Sentinel Rock
7,038'

overlook •

radio tower

63

32

Sentinel Fall

POHONO TR

Sentinel Dome
8,122'

60

Taft Point
7,503'

59

POHONO TR

TAFT POINT TR

Glacier Point Rd

59
60
61
P

N
W — E
S

To Inspiration Point
(Hike 53)

To Wawona Road

ALSO SEE MAPS ON
PAGES 140 • 153 • 155 • 159

61.
Pohono Trail Loop
TAFT POINT to SENTINEL DOME

trail as it gains elevation between the cliffs and the west slope of Sentinel Dome. A couple of switchbacks lead up to the base of the dome and a trail fork. The left fork leads to Glacier Point (Hike 62). Go to the right, passing a radio tower on the left. Curve around the north side of Sentinel Dome to an old road at a trail fork. The right fork climbs up the dome (Hike 60). After enjoying the panoramic views from atop the dome, continue south on the old abandoned road along the east end of Sentinel Dome. Follow the wide, sandy path downhill through open stands of evergreens and granite slabs. Cross a stream on a foot-bridge and return to the trailhead.

62. Glacier Point

Hiking distance: 0.6 miles round trip
Hiking time: 30 minutes
Elevation gain: Level
Maps: U.S.G.S. Half Dome
       Glacier Point Trail map

Summary of hike: Glacier Point is perched on the sheer southern wall of Yosemite Valley at an elevation of 7,214 feet. This short, wheelchair-accessible trail leads to some of the most inspiring vistas you may ever see. Several overhanging platforms provide spectacular views from 3,200 feet above the valley. The eagle's-eye view spreads out in every direction across the valley, highlighted by polished domes, snow-covered peaks, glacially carved valleys, four waterfalls, and the vast expanse of the High Sierra. A geology exhibit in an elevated gazebo-like rock enclosure explains the natural processes that formed the valley.

Driving directions: From the west end of Yosemite Valley, drive 9 miles south on Wawona Road/Highway 41 to Glacier Point Road. Turn left (east) on Glacier Point Road, and continue 15.7 miles to the Glacier Point parking lot at the end of the road.

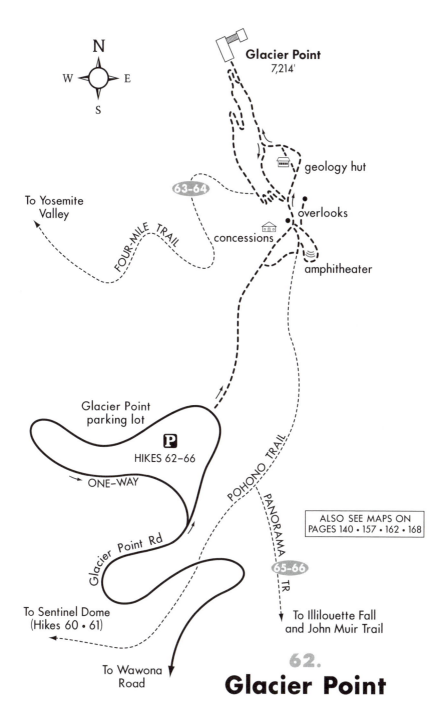

N
W   E
S

Glacier Point
7,214'

geology hut

63-64

overlooks

To Yosemite
Valley

FOUR-MILE TRAIL

concessions

amphitheater

Glacier Point
parking lot

P

HIKES 62–66

ONE-WAY

POHONO TRAIL

PANORAMA TR

ALSO SEE MAPS ON
PAGES 140 • 157 • 162 • 168

Glacier Point Rd

65-66

To Sentinel Dome
(Hikes 60 • 61)

To Illilouette Fall
and John Muir Trail

62.

To Wawona
Road

Glacier Point

Hiking directions: Take the paved Glacier Point Trail, passing the Panorama and Pohono Trails on the right and concessions on the left. Pass the site of the old Glacier Point Hotel (destroyed by fire in 1969) to a magnificent overlook of the High Sierra and Yosemite Valley. A geographic map identifies the many landmark formations, waterfalls, mountain peaks, and valleys. From the overlook, bear left to a 3-way split. To the left is the Four-Mile Trail (Hikes 63 and 64); the center fork leads directly to Glacier Point. Take the right fork to the geology hut in a rock enclosure, which includes interpretive panels and a reference map of the staggering views. Beyond the exhibit, the path rejoins the main trail. Go to the right towards Glacier Point, passing a connector trail to the Four-Mile Trail on the left. From the upper terrace by Overhanging Rock are views into and across Yosemite Valley. To the right, steps lead down to the lower terrace, with additional views across the east end of the valley.

63. Four-Mile Trail
GLACIER POINT along UPPER RIM

Hiking distance: 1.5 miles round trip
Hiking time: 1 hour
Elevation gain: 200 feet
Maps: U.S.G.S. Half Dome

map
page 162

Summary of hike: The Four-Mile Trail was the original route from Yosemite Valley to Glacier Point before Glacier Point Road was built. The trail, since designated for horse and foot traffic only, was rebuilt in the 1920s and is now 4.6 miles. This hike follows a short, easy section of the trail from Glacier Point along the upper south rim of the valley. The trail overlooks the sculptured landscape of Yosemite Valley from an elevation of 7,200 feet, with clear vantage points of the valley's natural landmarks. The scenic trail provides spectacular views of the eastern and western ends of the valley. Hike 64—a shuttle hike—continues down the trail to the valley floor.

Driving directions:

From the west end of Yosemite Valley, drive 9 miles south on Wawona Road/Highway 41 to Glacier Point Road. Turn left (east) on Glacier Point Road, and continue 15.7 miles to the Glacier Point parking lot at the end of the road.

Hiking directions:

Sentinel Rock along the Four-Mile Trail
7,038'

Take the paved path towards Glacier Point, passing the Panorama and Pohono Trails on the right. Curve left around the concession building, overlooking Yosemite Valley, Half Dome, North Dome, Tenaya Canyon, Vernal Fall, Nevada Fall, and the High Sierra peaks, to a posted trail split. The geology exhibit is to the right, and Glacier Point is straight ahead. Take the Four-Mile Trail to the left and descend to the dirt path. Leave the hordes of people behind, and walk downward into the quiet of the sugar pine and white fir forest. The first half mile offers continual vistas of the magnificent granite walls of Yosemite Valley. Curry Village and the Merced River can be seen far below on the valley floor. The cliff-hugging path curves left to a full view of the entire 2,425-foot Yosemite Falls and the vertical wall of El Capitan. Moderately descend, trying to focus on the trail instead of the stunning vistas. At 0.75 miles, curve around the contours of the cliffs to new westward views of Sentinel Rock and far down to the opposite end of Yosemite Valley. This is the turn-around spot.

Beyond this point, the trail begins a steep descent to the valley floor. For a 4.6-mile one-way shuttle hike, continue with Hike 64 to the valley floor.

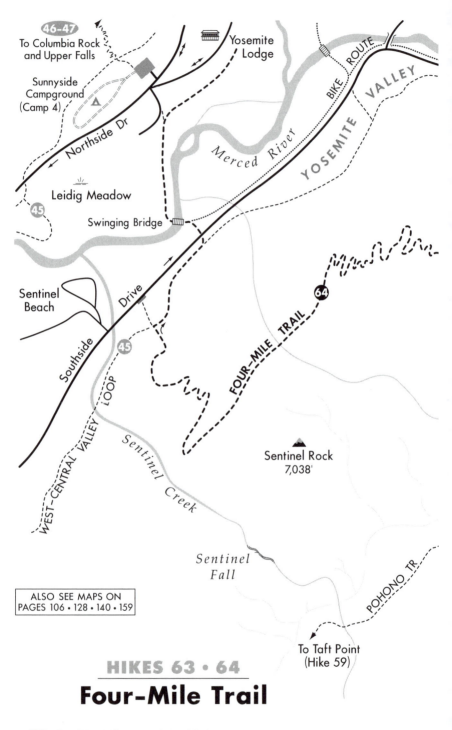

46-47

To Columbia Rock
and Upper Falls

Sunnyside
Campground
(Camp 4)

Northside Dr

Yosemite
Lodge

BIKE ROUTE

YOSEMITE VALLEY

Merced River

Leidig Meadow

45

Swinging Bridge

Sentinel
Beach

Drive

64

FOUR-MILE TRAIL

45

Southside

WEST–CENTRAL VALLEY LOOP

Sentinel Creek

Sentinel Rock
7,038'

Sentinel
Fall

POHONO TR.

ALSO SEE MAPS ON
PAGES 106 • 128 • 140 • 159

To Taft Point
(Hike 59)

HIKES 63 • 64
Four-Mile Trail

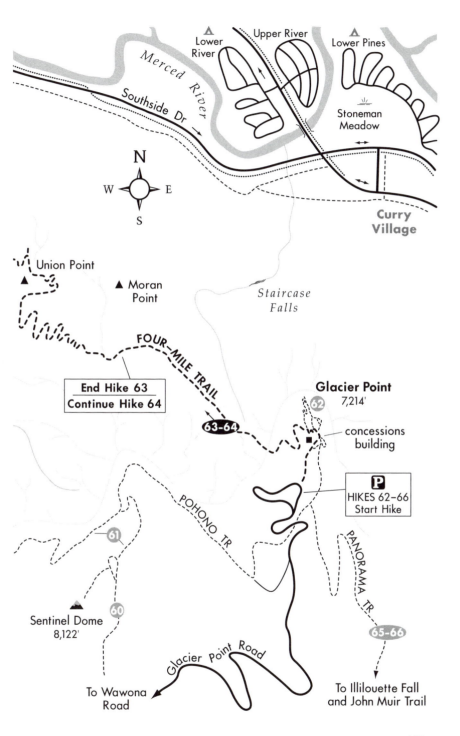

Lower River

Upper River

Lower Pines

Merced River

Southside Dr

Stoneman Meadow

N
W · E
S

Curry Village

Union Point

Moran Point

Staircase Falls

FOUR-MILE TRAIL

Glacier Point
7,214'

End Hike 63
Continue Hike 64

62

concessions building

63-64

P
HIKES 62–66
Start Hike

POHONO TR

61

PANORAMA TR

Sentinel Dome
8,122'

60

65-66

Glacier Point Road

To Wawona Road

To Illilouette Fall and John Muir Trail

64. Four-Mile Trail (shuttle)

Hiking distance: 5.2-mile one-way shuttle to Yosemite Lodge
Hiking time: 2.5 hours
Elevation loss: 3,200 feet
Maps: U.S.G.S. Half Dome

map
page 162

Summary of hike: The Four-Mile Trail connects Glacier Point atop Yosemite Valley's south rim to the valley floor. This hike follows the trail as it descends 3,200 feet over 4.6 miles, zigzagging down the cliffside. The hike begins with eastward views of Little Yosemite Valley, Nevada Fall, Vernal Fall, Liberty Cap, Half Dome, and Tenaya Canyon. Along the way the views open down to the west end of the valley and includes Sentinel Rock, Cathedral Rocks, El Capitan, Yosemite Falls, Royal Arches, and the Merced River. For a quicker and easier trail option, Hike 63 turns around just before the steep descent to the valley floor.

Driving directions: Take the shuttle bus from Yosemite Lodge or the Ahwahnee Hotel (leaving three times daily) one-way to Glacier Point.

Hiking directions: Follow the hiking directions for Hike 63 to its turn-around point, just before the steep descent to the valley floor. Continue down the Four-Mile Trail. There are no trail junctions. Switchback down the mountain to the valley floor. Once you begin the descent along the cliff, angling down into the valley, it is a continuous visual treat. Use Sentinel Rock, which is frequently in view, as a gauge to measure the descent. Reach a 4-way junction just shy of Southside Drive. Bear right a short distance and cross the road to the Merced River. Cross the river on Swinging Bridge and continue through Leidig Meadow back to the lodge.

65. Panorama Trail to Illilouette Fall

Hiking distance: 4 miles round trip
Hiking time: 2 hours
Elevation gain: 1,300 feet
Maps: U.S.G.S. Half Dome

**map
page 168**

Summary of hike: The Panorama Trail fulfills its name with spectacular bird's-eye views of the entire east end of Yosemite Valley. The trail begins at Glacier Point on the south rim of Yosemite Valley, passes Illilouette Fall, and continues to Nevada Fall and the John Muir Trail. This hike follows the first section of the trail to Illilouette Fall, which drops 370 feet over a granite lip and plummets down the deep vertical rock gorge, crashing onto the rocks below. Above the falls, Illilouette Creek cascades over large flat slabs of granite rock. The stunning geological features visible from the trail include Nevada, Vernal and Illilouette Falls; North Dome; Basket Dome; Half Dome; Clouds Rest; Mount Broderick; and Liberty Cap.

Driving directions: From the west end of Yosemite Valley, drive 9 miles south on Wawona Road/Highway 41 to Glacier Point Road. Turn left (east) on Glacier Point Road, and continue 15.7 miles to the Glacier Point parking lot at the end of the road.

Hiking directions: Take the paved Glacier Point Trail 70 yards to the posted trail on the right for the Panorama and Pohono Trails. Bear right and ascend the hill 0.1 mile to a Y-fork. The Pohono Trail bears right to Sentinel Dome and Taft Point (Hikes 60 and 59). Take the Panorama Trail to the left, and follow the cliff-side path overlooking Nevada Fall, Vernal Fall, and Half Dome. Gradually descend the wooded east slope of Illilouette Ridge on two long, sweeping switchbacks as views open up to Illilouette Gorge and Illilouette Fall. Traverse the mountainside, crossing numerous trickling streams while marveling at the ever-changing landscape. At the south end of the traverse is a posted junction. The right fork leads 4.3 miles to Mono Meadow (Hike 58). Bear left down a series of switchbacks into Illilouette Gorge. The thunderous sound of Illilouette Fall can be heard. At the last switchback is an overlook on the left of the waterfall, tucked into the deep gorge. Descend to the raging waters of Illilouette Creek. Follow the creek a hundred yards downstream under the shade of evergreens to an 80-foot metal bridge spanning the creek above the falls. This is the turn-around spot.

Hike 66 continues down the Panorama Trail to Nevada Fall, connecting with the John Muir Trail to Yosemite Valley for an 8.5-mile one-way shuttle hike.

66. Panorama Trail to Nevada Fall and John Muir Trail (shuttle)

Hiking distance: 8.5-mile one-way shuttle
Hiking time: 4 hours
Elevation loss: 3,200 feet
   (gaining 750 feet en route)
Maps: U.S.G.S. Half Dome

map
page 168

Summary of hike: This 8.5-mile one-way shuttle hike at the east end of Yosemite Valley descends 3,200 feet from Glacier Point atop the south rim of the valley to Happy Isles on the valley floor. From Glacier Point, the route traverses down Illilouette Ridge to the top of Illilouette Fall (Hike 65), crosses a bridge over the gorge, and follows along Panorama Cliff to Nevada Fall (Hike 52). The trail joins the John Muir Trail, following the watercourse of the Merced River back to the valley. Along the trail are stunning vistas of Yosemite Valley and several of its major geological features.

Driving directions: Take the shuttle bus from Yosemite Lodge or the Ahwahnee Hotel (leaving three times daily) one-way to Glacier Point.

If driving, park a shuttle car in the valley at the Curry Village parking lot. Then, from the west end of Yosemite Valley, drive 9 miles south on Wawona Road/Highway 41 to Glacier Point Road. Turn left (east) on Glacier Point Road, and continue 15.7 miles to the Glacier Point parking lot.

Hiking directions: Follow the hiking directions for Hike 65 to the bridge spanning Illilouette Creek just above Illilouette Fall. Cross the bridge and curve left on the Panorama Trail. Switchbacks zigzag up the forested hillside, ascending the west slope to Panorama Point. Notice the observation platforms back at Glacier Point. Continue uphill, gaining 750 feet along the edge of Panorama Cliff while overlooking Yosemite Valley, North Dome, Basket Dome, and Royal Arches. Leave the edge of the cliff, head into the forest, then return to views of Half Dome, Clouds Rest, Mount Broderick, and Liberty Cap. Pass a junction to Ottaway Lake on the right. Begin descending on a series of switchbacks towards Nevada Fall and a T-junction with the John Muir Trail at 5 miles.

From the John Muir Trail junction are several options to return down to the valley. (Every route descends and is filled with magnificent views.) The right fork leads 0.2 miles to the bridge crossing the Merced River at the brink of Nevada Fall. On this route, return on the Mist Trail along the north side of the river. Reference Hike 52.

Another option is to take the left fork on the John Muir Trail (the return route of Hike 52). One mile downhill along the John Muir Trail is a trail fork at Clark Point. To the right, the Clark Trail zigzags down to Vernal Fall and a T-junction with the Mist Trail. The left fork on the Mist Trail follows the south edge of the Merced River Canyon, passing Emerald Pool and Vernal Fall to the Vernal Fall Bridge.

Back at Clark Point, a third option is to take the left fork and stay on the John Muir Trail. Descend to the Vernal Fall Bridge, where the John Muir Trail and the Mist Trail unite. Cross the bridge and descend 0.8 miles to Happy Isles on the valley floor.

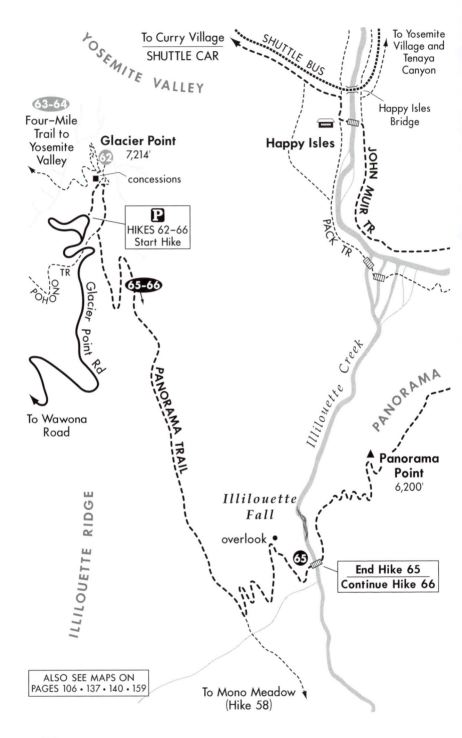

To Curry Village
SHUTTLE CAR

SHUTTLE BUS

To Yosemite
Village and
Tenaya
Canyon

YOSEMITE VALLEY

Happy Isles
Bridge

63-64
Four–Mile
Trail to
Yosemite
Valley

Glacier Point
7,214'

62

concessions

Happy Isles

JOHN MUIR TR

P
HIKES 62–66
Start Hike

POHONO TR

Glacier Point Rd

PACK TR

65-66

To Wawona
Road

PANORAMA TRAIL

PANORAMA

Illilouette Creek

▲ **Panorama Point**
6,200'

Illilouette Fall

overlook •

65

End Hike 65
Continue Hike 66

ILLILOUETTE RIDGE

ALSO SEE MAPS ON
PAGES 106 • 137 • 140 • 159

To Mono Meadow
(Hike 58)

N W E S

Half Dome
8,836'

Mt Broderick
6,706'

Grizzly Peak
6,222'

Vernal Fall

Silver Apron and Emerald Pool

Liberty Cap
7,076'

LITTLE YOSEMITE VALLEY

Vernal Fall Bridge

Merced River

MIST TRAIL

MIST TRAIL

To Half Dome

CLARK TR

Nevada Fall

observation platform

Clark Point

JOHN MUIR TRAIL

John Muir Trail junction

CLIFF

66 PANORAMA TRAIL

To Ottaway Lake

To Mono Meadow
(Hike 58)

Panorama Trail

HIKE 65
Illilouette Fall

HIKE 66
Nevada Fall • John Muir Shuttle

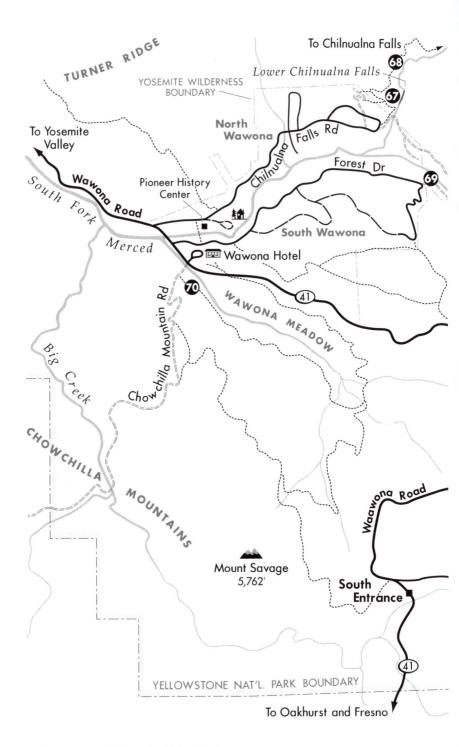

To Chilnualna Falls

68

Lower Chilnualna Falls

67

YOSEMITE WILDERNESS
BOUNDARY

TURNER RIDGE

**North
Wawona**

To Yosemite
Valley

Chilnualna Falls Rd

Forest Dr

69

Wawona Road

Pioneer History
Center

South Fork

Merced

South Wawona

Wawona Hotel

70

Chowchilla Mountain Rd

41

WAWONA MEADOW

Big Creek

CHOWCHILLA MOUNTAINS

Mount Savage
5,762'

Waawona Road

**South
Entrance**

41

YELLOWSTONE NAT'L. PARK BOUNDARY

To Oakhurst and Fresno

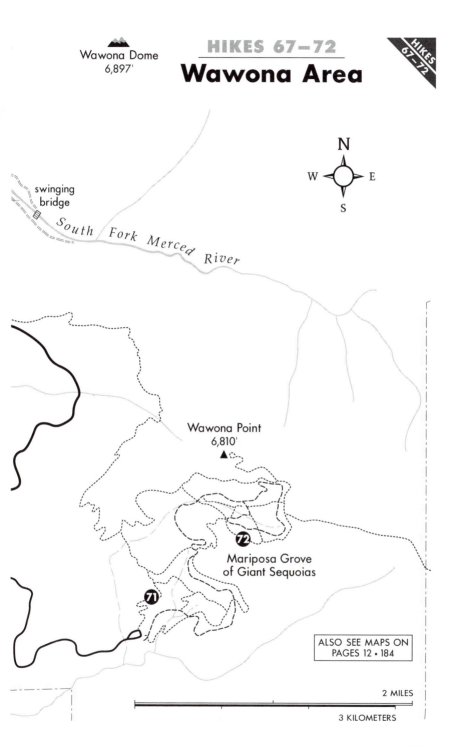

Wawona Area

Wawona Dome
6,897'

N
W · E
S

swinging
bridge

South Fork Merced River

Wawona Point
6,810'
▲

72

Mariposa Grove
of Giant Sequoias

71

ALSO SEE MAPS ON
PAGES 12 · 184

2 MILES

3 KILOMETERS

67. Lower Chilnualna Falls

Hiking distance: 1-mile loop
Hiking time: 30 minutes
Elevation gain: 300 feet
Maps: U.S.G.S. Wawona

Summary of hike: Lower Chilnualna Falls is a multi-tiered 25-foot cataract that roars through a narrow granite canyon with a tremendous volume of water. The trail parallels Chilnualna Creek along a furious whitewater cascade tumbling over room-sized boulders. It is a wonderful spot to sit and watch the magnificent water display from the surrounding granite slabs and boulders.

Driving directions: From the Wawona Hotel at the south end of the park, take Wawona Road/Highway 41 a quarter mile north to Chilnualna Falls Road. It is located on the north side of the bridge that crosses the South Fork Merced River. Turn right and follow Chilnualna Falls Road 1.7 miles to the signed trailhead parking area on the right.

Hiking directions: Walk up the paved road 0.1 mile to a posted road fork. Bear left ten yards to a second trail fork. The left fork is the stock route to Chilnualna Falls (Hike 68). Curve right on the footpath, and climb the hillside along the thunderous cascades of Chilnualna Creek. A steep path descends to the creek through a forest of redwood, oak and ponderosa pine. A short distance ahead is an overlook of Lower Chilnualna Falls. Climb granite stairsteps along the raging watercourse, marveling at the powerful water display. A short spur trail continues to a meeting of the rock cliffs and the creek. Return to the main trail, and climb away from the creek up the oak-covered hillside, reaching a junction with the stock route on the left. Go to the right on the Chilnualna Falls Trail. Weave through the forest, with vistas of Wawona Valley, Turner Ridge, and Mount Savage. At the trail fork, the right fork continues on the Chilnualna Falls Trail (Hike 68). Take the unpaved road to the left, which becomes Larke Street, and head downhill through the east edge of North Wawona to Chilnualna Falls Road. Bear left, returning to the parking area.

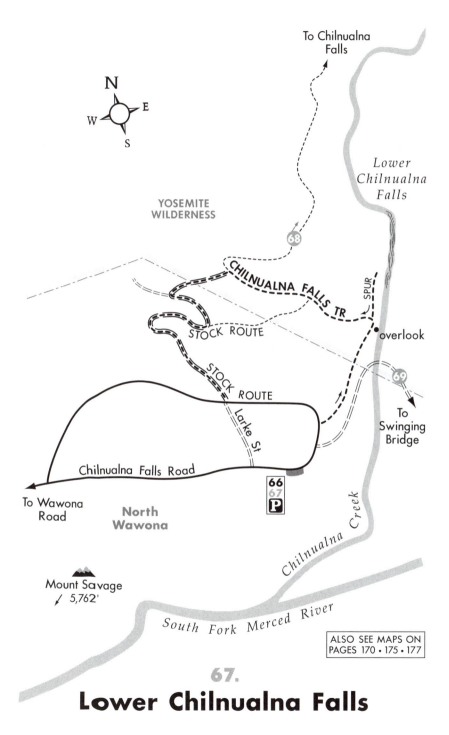

To Chilnualna
Falls

N
E
W
S

YOSEMITE
WILDERNESS

*Lower
Chilnualna
Falls*

68

CHILNUALNA FALLS TR

SPUR

STOCK ROUTE

overlook

STOCK ROUTE

69

To
Swinging
Bridge

Larke St

Chilnualna Falls Road

66
67
P

To Wawona
Road

**North
Wawona**

Chilnualna Creek

Mount Savage
5,762'

South Fork Merced River

ALSO SEE MAPS ON
PAGES 170 • 175 • 177

67.
Lower Chilnualna Falls

68. Chilnualna Falls

Hiking distance: 8.2 miles round trip
Hiking time: 4.5 hours
Elevation gain: 2,400 feet
Maps: U.S.G.S. Wawona and Mariposa Falls

Summary of hike: Chilnualna Falls twists through a narrow rock chasm and freefalls 240 feet down a narrow gorge from high above the Wawona basin. Above the main falls, a cataract tumbles another 60 feet in a series of cascades separated by pools and large granite slabs. This trail heads up switchbacks that steadily climb to the top of the falls, gaining 2,400 feet in four miles. At the top, granite steps follow the creek past the numerous pools and cascades. Along the trail are magnificent views of the forested Wawona area and the Chowchilla Mountains.

Driving directions: Same as Hike 67.

Hiking directions: Walk up the paved road 0.1 mile to a posted road fork. Bear left ten yards to a second trail fork. The left fork is the stock route. The right fork follows Chilnualna Creek past Lower Chilnualna Falls (Hike 67). Take either route, as both routes merge ahead. Continue uphill on the Chilnualna Falls Trail through an oak, pine, and incense cedar forest, entering the Yosemite Wilderness. Curving east, the trail reaches Chilnualna Creek and briefly parallels it up canyon. Curve away from the creek, and ascend a series of long, wide switchbacks. Cross a couple of small seasonal streams while the undergrowth changes to manzanita, deer brush, and bear clover. The views alternate between westward vistas of Wawona Valley and the Chowchilla Mountains and eastward vistas of Wawona Dome. At two miles, reach a granite plateau with an overlook of the tree-filled canyon and Wawona Dome, towering over the valley directly to the east. A half mile beyond the overlook is a glimpse of the tumbling waterfall high up on the canyon wall. The switchbacks continue uphill, opening to more views of the cataract's length. At 3 miles, rock hop over a small stream, and enter a forest of incense cedar and sugar pine. Cross a gully and traverse the face of a cliff on a near-level ledge overlooking the freefalling lower end of Chilnualna Falls. From the brink of the falls, a granite stair path follows the creek past a series of cascades connected by pools. This is a great spot to rest and enjoy the creek. At the uppermost cascade is a posted junction, the turn-around point.

The left fork continues to Bridalveil Campground, connecting with Hike 57. The right fork continues to Buck Camp.

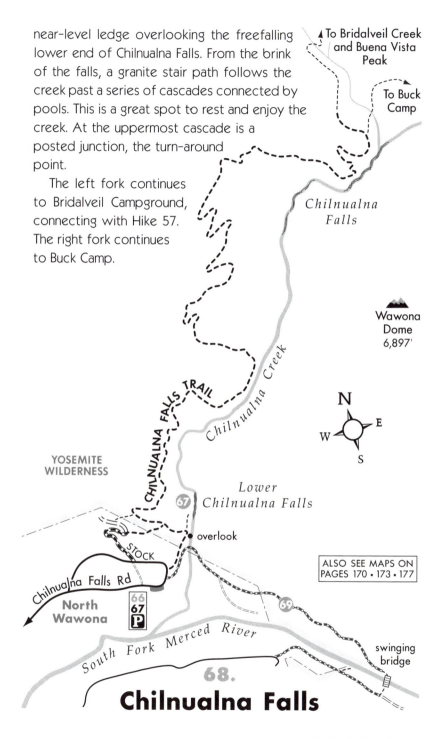

To Bridalveil Creek and Buena Vista Peak

To Buck Camp

Chilnualna Falls

Wawona Dome 6,897'

Chilnualna Creek

N
W · E
S

CHILNUALNA FALLS TRAIL

YOSEMITE WILDERNESS

Lower Chilnualna Falls

67

overlook

STOCK

ALSO SEE MAPS ON PAGES 170 · 173 · 177

Chilnualna Falls Rd

North Wawona

66
67
P

69

South Fork Merced River

swinging bridge

68.
Chilnualna Falls

69. Swinging Bridge Trail

Hiking distance: 1.8 miles round trip or 4.7-mile loop
Hiking time: 30 minutes or 2 hours
Elevation gain: Level
Maps: U.S.G.S. Wawona and Mariposa Grove

Summary of hike: The swinging bridge spans the South Fork Merced River near Wawona. It is a wooden plank and cable bridge mounted on granite rock. A trail parallels the north and south banks of the river along whitewater cascades. The hike can be enjoyed as a short stroll to the bridge or as a four-mile loop. The loop connects Forest Drive with Chilnualna Falls Road, recrossing the river on a covered bridge by the Pioneer History Center.

Driving directions: From Wawona Hotel at the south end of the park, take Wawona Road/Highway 41 north 0.1 mile to Forest Drive, just before crossing the bridge over the South Fork Merced River. Turn right and continue 1.8 miles to a road fork by a rock wall and Camp Wawona. Curve left on the unpaved road, and drive a quarter mile to the signed trailhead at a trail gate. Park in the area on the left.

Hiking directions: Walk past the trailhead gate, and follow the unpaved forest road east. Parallel the South Fork Merced River upstream. A side path on the left leads down to the river by flat, granite slabs and slow, circling eddies. From the river, the swinging bridge can be seen upstream. Return to the main trail and continue upstream to the bridge. Cross the swinging bridge to the north banks of the river. The path, a dirt road, heads downstream and curves away from the riverbank. The dirt road becomes Chilnualna Falls Road by the trailhead for Chilnualna Falls (Hikes 67 and 68). For a 0.6-mile round trip hike, retrace your steps back to the parking lot.

For a 4-mile loop, follow Chilnualna Falls Road west through the small town of North Wawona to the horse stables and Pioneer History Center on the left. Cross the covered bridge spanning the South Fork Merced River, returning to Forest Drive.

Bear left and complete the loop on the road back to the parking area.

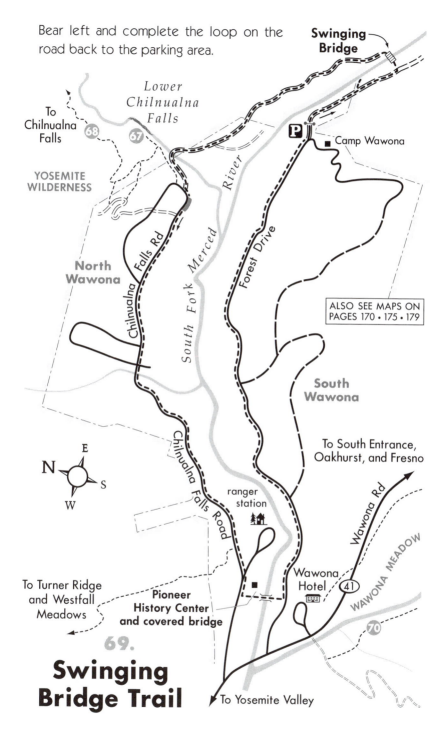

Swinging Bridge

Lower Chilnualna Falls

To Chilnualna Falls 68 37

Camp Wawona

YOSEMITE WILDERNESS

North Wawona

Chilnualna Falls Rd

South Fork Merced River

Forest Drive

ALSO SEE MAPS ON PAGES 170 • 175 • 179

South Wawona

To South Entrance, Oakhurst, and Fresno

N E S W

ranger station

Chilnualna Falls Road

Wawona Rd

To Turner Ridge and Westfall Meadows

Pioneer History Center and covered bridge

Wawona Hotel 41

WAWONA MEADOW

70

69.

Swinging Bridge Trail

To Yosemite Valley

70. Wawona Meadow Loop
from WAWONA HOTEL

Hiking distance: 3.5-mile loop
Hiking time: 2 hours
Elevation gain: 200 feet
Maps: U.S.G.S. Wawona

Summary of hike: The Wawona Hotel is a beautiful Victorian complex originally constructed in 1876. It now comprises six stately buildings with wide porches and is surrounded by expansive green lawns. Wawona Meadow, a mile-long pastoral meadow rimmed with ponderosa pine, oak and cedar, sits in the Wawona basin across the road from the hotel. This hike follows an old road that circles the edge of the meadow along the base of Mount Savage. At the lower west end of the meadow is the well-groomed Wawona Golf Course, dating back to 1917. At this low 4,000-foot elevation, the meadow loop can be hiked year-round.

Driving directions: Park in the lot for the Wawona Hotel at the south end of the park on Wawona Road/Highway 41. The trailhead is directly across the highway from the hotel.

Hiking directions: From the parking lot at the Wawona Hotel, cross Wawona Road to the paved path. Follow the path through the Wawona Golf Course to the posted Meadow Loop. Bear left past the trailhead gate, quickly leaving the golf course behind. Head east along the forested foothills of Mount Savage on the unpaved road. Stroll through the shade of oak, ponderosa pine, and incense cedar while overlooking Wawona Meadow. Cross a fern-lined stream, and follow the south edge of the meadow along the forest floor, parallel to an old split rail fence that once confined grazing cattle and sheep. At the southeast end of the meadow, cross a series of three trickling streams. After the second stream crossing is an unsigned trail on the right that heads to Mount Savage. Rock hop over the third stream and begin the return. Follow the north edge of the meadow to a trail gate by Wawona Road at 3.2 miles. Continue on the footpath parallel to and below the road. Cross to the north side of Wawona Road and return to the Wawona Hotel.

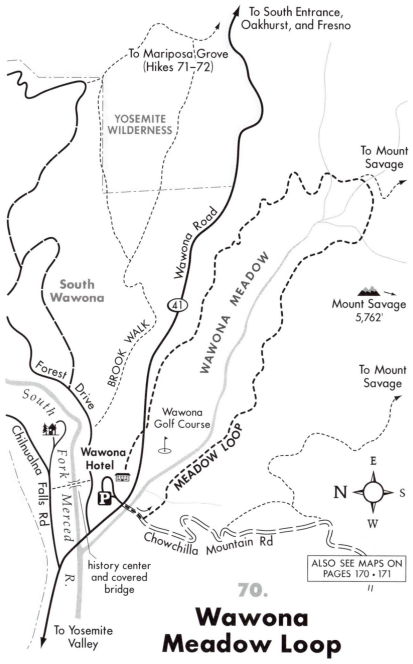

To South Entrance, Oakhurst, and Fresno

To Mariposa Grove (Hikes 71–72)

YOSEMITE WILDERNESS

To Mount Savage

Wawona Road

South Wawona

WAWONA MEADOW

BROOK WALK

41

Mount Savage 5,762'

Forest Drive

To Mount Savage

South

Wawona Golf Course

MEADOW LOOP

Chilnualna Falls Rd

Fork Merced R.

Wawona Hotel

P

E
N — S
W

Chowchilla Mountain Rd

history center and covered bridge

ALSO SEE MAPS ON PAGES 170 · 171

70.

Wawona Meadow Loop

To Yosemite Valley

Mariposa Grove of Giant Sequoias

HIKES 71 and 72

Summary of hike: Yosemite National Park has three giant sequoia groves. Of these three, the Mariposa Grove of Giant Sequoias is the largest and most visited. It is divided into two groves—Upper Grove and Lower Grove. Some of these giant sequoias are believed to be nearly 3,000 years old. Their average height is 250 feet, with a base diameter of 15 to 20 feet and bark that is two feet thick. Their shallow roots are only 3 to 6 feet deep but extend outwards up to 150 feet to support the massive trees. Sequoias are among the oldest and largest living things on earth and are resistant to disease, insects and fire.

Mariposa Grove has an impressive display of more than 300 mature giant sequoias within its 250-acre area. One of the largest and oldest trees in this grove is the Grizzly Giant, estimated to be 2,700 years old with a height of 200 feet and a 30-foot diameter. Although the grove is dominated by giant sequoias, there is a forested mix of ponderosa pine, sugar pine, white fir, black oak, and incense cedar.

The area has a network of trails that crisscross the grove, offering a variety of routes. **Hike 71** explores the Lower Grove only. It is 2.2 miles round trip with a 400-foot elevation gain. Information plaques are placed along the trail. The trail visits the Grizzly Giant, California Tunnel Tree, Fallen Monarch, The Bachelor, and Three Graces.

Hike 72 utilizes the tram up to the Mariposa Grove Museum in the Upper Grove. From the Upper Grove, it is a one-way, 2.5-mile return walk that descends a thousand feet through both groves back to the parking lot. This trail includes all of the trees in the first hike, plus the Fallen Wawona Tree, Telescope Tree, Columbia Tree, Clothespin Tree, and Faithful Couple. The hike also allows a visit to the museum and a quiet walk through the forest. Whichever hike or side trails are chosen, the area is beautiful and rewarding.

Driving and hiking directions are found on the next page.

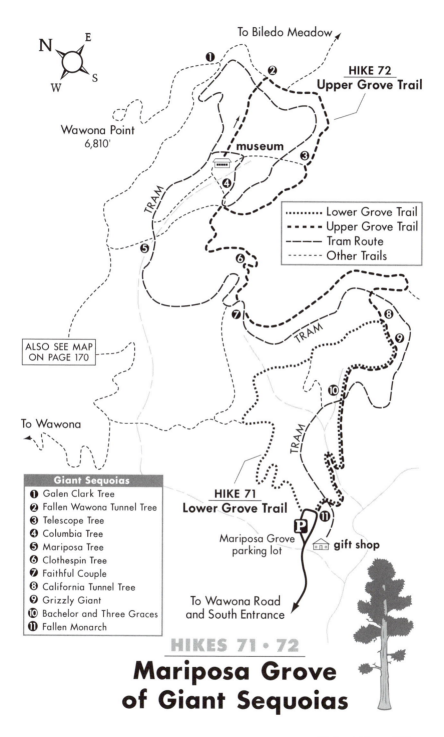

N E W S

To Biledo Meadow

HIKE 72
Upper Grove Trail

Wawona Point
6,810'

museum

❶

❷

❸

❹

❺

❻

❼

❽

❾

.... Lower Grove Trail
▪▪▪▪ Upper Grove Trail
— — Tram Route
- - - Other Trails

TRAM

TRAM

ALSO SEE MAP
ON PAGE 170

To Wawona

TRAM

❿

⓫

Giant Sequoias
❶ Galen Clark Tree
❷ Fallen Wawona Tunnel Tree
❸ Telescope Tree
❹ Columbia Tree
❺ Mariposa Tree
❻ Clothespin Tree
❼ Faithful Couple
❽ California Tunnel Tree
❾ Grizzly Giant
❿ Bachelor and Three Graces
⓫ Fallen Monarch

HIKE 71
Lower Grove Trail

P

🏠 gift shop

Mariposa Grove
parking lot

To Wawona Road
and South Entrance

HIKES 71 • 72
Mariposa Grove
of Giant Sequoias

71. Lower Mariposa Grove

Hiking distance: 2.2-mile loop
Hiking time: 1 hour
Elevation gain: 400 feet
Maps: U.S.G.S. Mariposa Grove
     Mariposa Grove of Giant Sequoias—Guide and Map

map
page 181

Driving directions: From the west end of Yosemite Valley, drive 28.5 miles south on Wawona Road/Highway 41 to the Mariposa Grove parking lot, staying to the left at the road fork by the south entrance. The parking lot is 6.8 miles past Wawona.

From the south entrance, turn right (east) and drive 2 miles to the Mariposa Grove parking lot at the end of the road.

A free shuttle to Mariposa Grove is available from Wawona.

Hiking directions: The Mariposa Grove map is on the previous page. This hike follows the Lower Grove Trail, hiking counterclockwise.

The trailhead is at the end of the parking lot next to the interpretive display and map dispenser. Take the trail a short distance to the Fallen Monarch tree, which toppled more than 300 years ago. After the Fallen Monarch is a footbridge and the tram road. Cross the road and continue gently uphill on the rock steps to a group of trees called The Bachelor and Three Graces. The Three Graces are grouped together while The Bachelor is off on its own. Again cross the tram road to the trail alongside a stream, and continue to the topped Grizzly Giant, with a circumference more than 100 feet. Circle the Grizzly Giant and head north about 50 yards to the California Tunnel Tree. A tunnel was cut through the tree in 1895 for the growing tourist industry. Take the northwest trail that leads to Wawona. At the second junction on the left, head back to the parking lot, completing the loop. (The first junction leads back to The Bachelor and Three Graces.)

72. Upper and Lower Mariposa Grove
via TRAM RIDE to MARIPOSA GROVE MUSEUM

Hiking distance: 2.5 miles one-way return
Hiking time: 1.5 hours, plus tram ride
Elevation loss: 1,000 feet
Maps: U.S.G.S. Mariposa Grove
      Mariposa Grove of Giant Sequoias—Guide and Map

map
page 181

Driving directions: Same as Hike 71.

Hiking directions: The Mariposa Grove map is on the previous page. This hike follows the Upper Grove Trail, starting at the museum and returning to the parking lot.

The open-air tram departs from the gift shop near the parking lot every 20 minutes. It winds 2.5 miles through the Lower Grove to the Upper Grove. The tram drivers stop along the way and share information about the trees and history of the area.

Depart the tram at the Mariposa Grove Museum. After visiting the museum, head east 0.3 miles to the Fallen Wawona Tunnel Tree at 6,600 feet, the high point of the hike. This tree was tunneled out for stage coaches in 1881 and toppled in 1969. Head south along the Outer Loop Trail down to the Telescope Tree, hollowed by fire yet still alive. You may gaze up to the sky through the hollowed trunk of the tree. Continue downhill to Columbia Tree, the tallest tree in the grove at 290 feet. At the nearby four-way junction, take the west trail downhill past Clothespin Tree to the tram road. The road is adjacent to Faithful Couple, two separate trees fused together at their bases. From here, go left along the tram road a short distance, and pick up the trail going to the east, which intersects with the Lower Grove Trail at Grizzly Giant and California Tunnel Tree. Continue west, passing The Bachelor, Three Graces, and Fallen Monarch back to the parking lot.

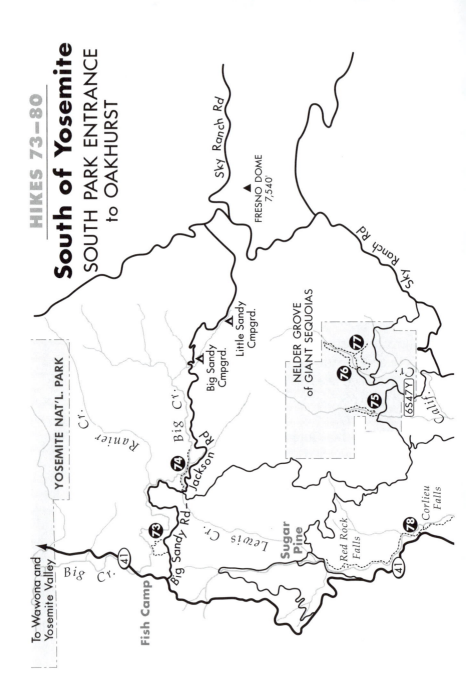

Sky Ranch Rd

FRESNO DOME
7,540'

Sky Ranch Rd

NELDER GROVE
of GIANT SEQUOIAS

77

76

75

6S47Y

Calif.

Little Sandy
Cmpgrd.

Big Sandy
Cmpgrd.

Big Cr.

Jackson Rd

74

Rainier Cr.

Cr.

YOSEMITE NAT'L. PARK

To Wawona and
Yosemite Valley

Big Cr.

41

Fish Camp

73

Big Sandy Rd.

Lewis Cr.

Sugar
Pine

Red Rock
Falls

41

78

Corlieu
Falls

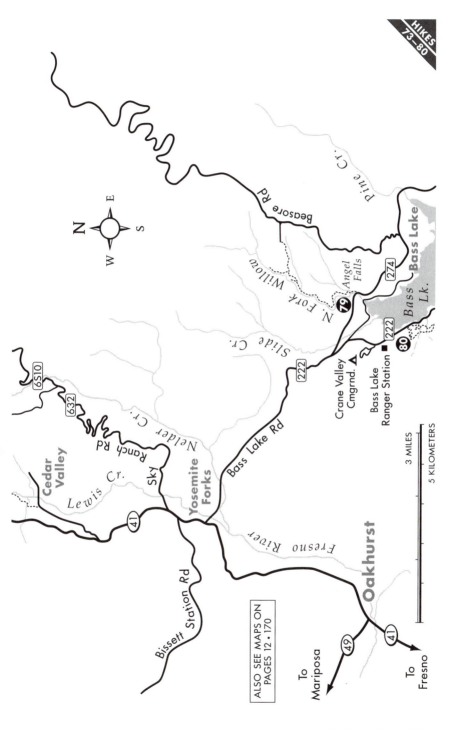

N
W E S

Pine Cr.

Beasore Rd

Bass Lake

N. Fork Willow

Angel Falls

274

79

Slide Cr.

222

Bass Lk.

222

Crane Valley Cmgrnd. △

Bass Lake Ranger Station ■

80

6S10

632

Nelder Cr.

Sky Ranch Rd

Lewis Cr.

Cedar Valley

Yosemite Forks

Bass Lake Rd

41

3 MILES

5 KILOMETERS

Fresno River

Oakhurst

Bissett Station Rd

ALSO SEE MAPS ON PAGES 12 • 170

49

To Mariposa

41

To Fresno

73. Tenaya Nature Trail

Hiking distance: 0.8 mile loop
Hiking time: 30 minutes
Elevation gain: 200 feet
Maps: U.S.G.S. Fish Camp

Summary of hike: The Tenaya Nature Trail is an easy and scenic loop between Big Sandy Road and the south banks of Big Creek, just south of Yosemite National Park and the town of Fish Camp. The name Tenaya comes from Chief Tenaya, a legendary Southern Sierra Miwok Indian chief from the early 19th century. The meandering path weaves through a mixed forest, a small sequoia grove, an open meadow, and follows along the banks of Big Creek.

Driving directions: From the south park entrance, drive 2.7 miles south on Highway 41 to the posted Big Sandy Road/ Jackson Road (just beyond Tenaya Lodge) and turn left. Proceed 0.7 miles on the narrow dirt road to the trail on the left, located 30 yards past the "Slow Horse and Wagon" sign. Park in the pull-outs on either side of the road.

From Oakhurst, drive 13 miles north on Highway 41 to the posted Big Sandy Road/Jackson Road and turn right. Continue with the directions above.

Hiking directions: Take the footpath on the north side of the road for 50 yards to a corral fence. Bear left and descend through a mixed evergreen forest and a groundcover of bracken ferns. Drop down into an open meadow, and pass a giant sequoia to a T-junction at Big Creek. The right fork leads to a bridge crossing the creek into a privately owned camp. Bear left and head downstream. Curve away from the creek and meander through the west side of the meadow. Ascend the hillside and reenter the red fir forest with a few random cedars and sequoias. A short distance ahead, the path returns to Jackson Road. Take the road a quarter mile to the left, completing the loop.

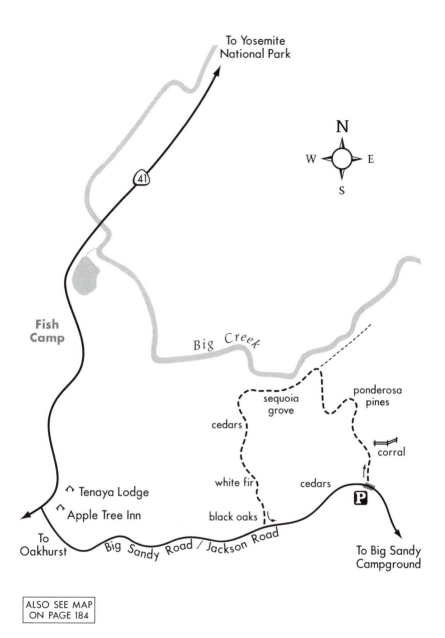

To Yosemite
National Park

N
W ← → E
S

41

**Fish
Camp**

Big Creek

sequoia
grove

ponderosa
pines

cedars

corral

white fir

cedars

⌂ Tenaya Lodge

⌂ Apple Tree Inn

black oaks

P

To
Oakhurst

Big Sandy Road / Jackson Road

To Big Sandy
Campground

ALSO SEE MAP
ON PAGE 184

73.
Tenaya Nature Trail

74. Tenaya Falls and Fish Camp Falls

Hiking distance: 1.6 miles round trip
Hiking time: 1 hour
Elevation gain: 50 feet
Maps: U.S.G.S. White Chief Mountain

Summary of hike: Big Creek forms in the upper slopes of White Chief Mountain in the Sierra National Forest just outside of Yosemite National Park. The creek joins the South Fork of the Merced River at Wawona. This short hike leads to three free-fall cataracts along Big Creek. The trail follows a water diversion ditch along a fern-lined rock grotto to 30-foot Fish Camp Falls, surrounded by smooth granite boulders; 20-foot Tenaya Falls; and an unnamed 25-foot waterfall. All three falls plunge into pools.

Driving directions: From the south park entrance, drive 2.7 miles south on Highway 41 to the posted Big Sandy Road/ Jackson Road (just beyond Tenaya Lodge) and turn left. Proceed 2.6 miles on the unpaved road to a small green water diversion structure on the left, just before the posted turnoff for Sugar Pine and Nelder Grove. Park in the pullouts on either side of the road by the post and rail fence.

From Oakhurst, drive 13 miles north on Highway 41 to the posted Big Sandy Road/Jackson Road and turn right. Continue with the directions above.

Hiking directions: Cross Jackson Road to the gated dirt road by the small metal structure. Pass the gate and follow the north edge of the water ditch. Pass an old wood bunkhouse and take the footpath on the narrow ridge. Head upstream along the ridge. The trail lies between the water ditch and a mossy vertical rock wall, situated on the right, and Big Creek, far below on the left. The creek can be seen running through a series of clear pools carved into the rock. In just over a half mile, where the water ditch and Big Creek split, 20-foot Tenaya Falls drops off a concrete spillway into a huge, deep pool. Just behind Tenaya Falls, across the creek on the south canyon wall, is the unnamed

25-foot, two-tiered waterfall with another pool.
(To get there requires wading across the creek.)

To reach Fish Camp Falls, cross the wall just
above Tenaya Falls, and continue upstream
along the north edge of Big Creek. A quarter
mile ahead is a slab rock formation with a
series of three rock-carved, stair-stepped
pools and gorgeous Fish Camp Falls.
After exploring the area, return
along the same trail.

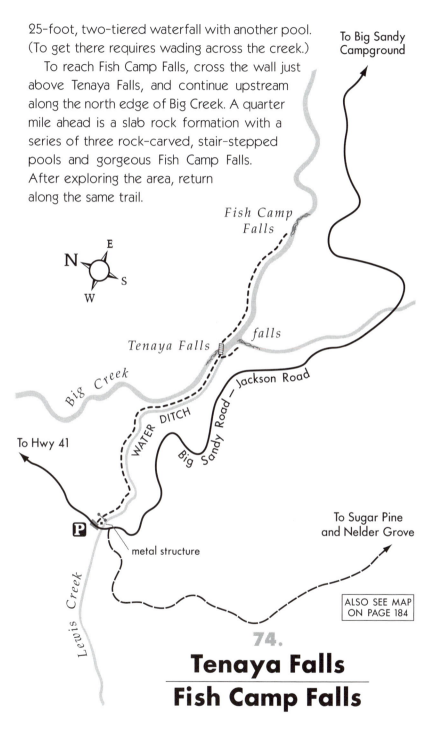

To Big Sandy
Campground

Fish Camp
Falls

N E W S

falls

Tenaya Falls

Big Creek

Jackson Road

WATER DITCH

Big Sandy Road

To Hwy 41

P

metal structure

To Sugar Pine
and Nelder Grove

Lewis Creek

ALSO SEE MAP
ON PAGE 184

74.

Tenaya Falls
Fish Camp Falls

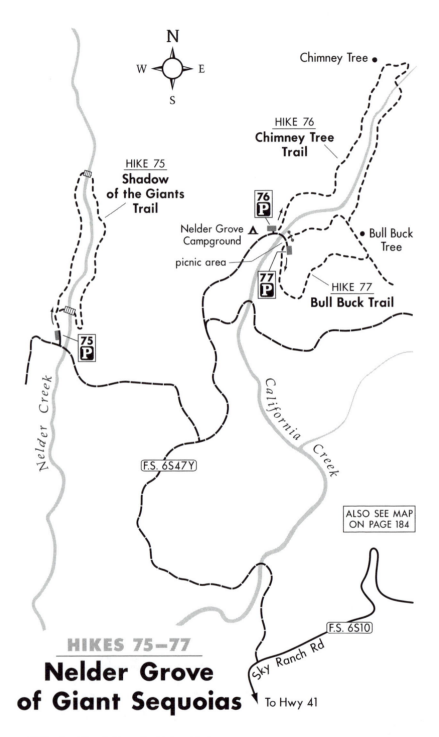

N

W   E

S

Chimney Tree ●

HIKE 76
**Chimney Tree
Trail**

HIKE 75
**Shadow
of the Giants
Trail**

76
P

Nelder Grove ▲
Campground

● Bull Buck
Tree

picnic area

77
P

HIKE 77
Bull Buck Trail

75
P

Nelder Creek

California Creek

F.S. 6S47Y

ALSO SEE MAP
ON PAGE 184

F.S. 6S10

HIKES 75–77
Nelder Grove
of Giant Sequoias

Sky Ranch Rd

To Hwy 41

75. Shadow of the Giants
NATIONAL RECREATION TRAIL
NELDER GROVE of GIANT SEQUOIAS

Hiking distance: 1.2-mile loop
Hiking time: 45 minutes
Elevation gain: 200 feet
Maps: U.S.G.S. White Chief Mountain

map
page 190

Summary of hike: The Nelder Grove Giant Sequoia Preservation Area is located due south of Yosemite's Mariposa Grove in the Sierra National Forest. The stately grove, named for a hermit that lived in the area, has giant sequoias as old as 3,000 years. The Shadow of the Giants National Recreation Trail is located in the southwest corner of Nelder Grove among some of the finest giant sequoia trees in the region. This historical grove was partially logged in the 1880s. Several massive stumps are scattered amongst the full-size giants.

The one-mile interpretive loop follows Nelder Creek and tells the story of the surrounding ecology. The tree species include giant sequoias, incense cedars, white fir, ponderosa pine, and sugar pines (known as the *King of the Pines*). The panels describe their life cycle, composition, root system, age, size, and the effects of fire, humans, and logging. This hike is an opportunity to see a grove of giant sequoias in a cool, quiet forest without the crowds of Yosemite.

Driving directions: From the south park entrance, drive 11.9 miles south on Highway 41 to Sky Ranch Road (Road 632) and turn left. Proceed 6.7 miles to the posted Nelder Grove turnoff. (En route, the road becomes Road 6S10.) Turn left onto Road 6S47Y, and continue 1.2 miles on the dirt road to a posted road split. Take the left fork and drive 0.6 miles to the Shadow of the Giants turnoff on the right. Park 60 yards ahead by the posted trailhead.

From Oakhurst, drive 3.7 miles north on Highway 41 to Sky Ranch Road (Road 632) and turn right. Continue with the directions above.

Hiking directions: Walk past the trailhead to the west bank of Nelder Creek in a lush, fern-filled forest. Head upstream along the creek from panel to panel. At the north end of the loop, the terrain is filled with giant sequoias. Cross a log bridge over Nelder Creek, and head downstream along the east bank. Follow the hillside above the creek, then cross another log bridge over the creek, completing the loop.

76. Chimney Tree Trail
NELDER GROVE of GIANT SEQUOIAS

Hiking distance: 1.5-mile loop
Hiking time: 40 minutes
Elevation gain: 200 feet
Maps: U.S.G.S. White Chief Mountain

map
page 190

Summary of hike: Chimney Tree is an amazing giant sequoia in Nelder Grove just south of Yosemite in the Sierra National Forest. The massive tree was hollowed out from fire, but it is still alive and healthy. It is possible to walk through the tree and see the sky through the chimney-like center. Several younger trees are growing within the chimney stack. The loop trail meanders along California Creek through a remote forest with scattered redwoods and second-growth pines, fir, and incense cedars.

Driving directions: From the south park entrance, drive 11.9 miles south on Highway 41 to Sky Ranch Road (Road 632) and turn left. Proceed 6.7 miles to the posted Nelder Grove turnoff. (En route, the road becomes Road 6S10.) Turn left onto Road 6S47Y, and continue 1.2 miles on the dirt road to a posted road split. Take the right fork and drive 0.5 miles, following the signs to Nelder Grove Campground. Just before entering the campground, park in the large pullout on the left by the signs for the campground and Chimney Tree Trail.

From Oakhurst, drive 3.7 miles north on Highway 41 to Sky Ranch Road (Road 632) and turn right. Continue with the directions above.

Hiking directions: Pass the posted trailhead into the mixed forest. Head north on the spongy path, carpeted with pine needles. Stroll under sugar pines, ponderosa pines, and incense cedars. At the north (upper) end of the loop are randomly scattered giant sequoias which dwarf the surrounding trees. The prominent Chimney Tree is on the left. After walking through and marveling at the giant, curve right. Pass a massive tree stump to California Creek. Follow the creek downstream and cross the log bridge over the fern-lined creek. Continue downhill, passing more giant sequoias and massive stumps to a T-junction with the Bull Buck Trail. A short distance to the left is the impressive Bull Buck Tree—Hike 77. Continue following the east bank of California Creek downstream to a metal gate. Pass the gate to the campground road. Bear right on the road, completing the loop by the campground entrance.

77. Bull Buck Trail
NELDER GROVE of GIANT SEQUOIAS

Hiking distance: 0.8-mile loop
Hiking time: 30 minutes
Elevation gain: 100 feet
Maps: U.S.G.S. White Chief Mountain

map
page 190

Summary of hike: The Nelder Grove of Giant Sequoias contains 106 mature giant sequoias scattered within a dense, 1,540-acre forest of pines, fir, and incense cedars. It is located in the center of the Sequoia Range, south of Yosemite National Park. The isolated grove was named after John Nelder, an old prospector who built a log cabin beneath the towering trees in 1875 and homesteaded the land. Bull Buck Tree, once considered the world's largest tree, stands 246 feet high with a base circumference of 99 feet. This loop hike follows the banks of California Creek and visits the giant tree, weaving through a mixed forest of cedars, pines, fir and huge, majestic redwoods. Within this historical grove is evidence of previous Native American occupation and the signs of extensive logging from the late 1800s.

Driving directions: From the south park entrance, drive 11.9 miles south on Highway 41 to Sky Ranch Road (Road 632) and turn left. Proceed 6.7 miles to the posted Nelder Grove turnoff. (En route, the road becomes Road 6S10.) Turn left onto Road 6S47Y, and continue 1.2 miles on the dirt road to a posted road split. Take the right fork and drive 0.6 miles, passing through the Nelder Grove Campground to the posted Bull Buck Trail on the right. Park at the trailhead.

From Oakhurst, drive 3.7 miles north on Highway 41 to Sky Ranch Road (Road 632) and turn right. Continue with the directions above.

Hiking directions: From the picnic area on the banks of California Creek, bear left on the posted trail. Stroll through the rolling hills in a forest of incense cedar, white fir, sugar pine, and dogwood to a T-junction. Bear left to the 2,700-year-old Bull Buck Tree on the right. After marveling at the impressive giant, continue past Bull Buck Tree to a junction with the Chimney Tree Trail (Hike 76) on the right. Head left, following the east bank of California Creek downstream to a metal gate. Pass the gate to the campground road. Bear left 100 yards back to the trailhead picnic area.

78. Lewis Creek
National Recreation Trail
to Corlieu Falls and Red Rock Falls

Hiking distance: 3.6 miles round trip
Hiking time: 2 hours
Elevation gain: 600 feet
Maps: U.S.G.S. Fish Camp and White Chief Mountain

Summary of hike: The Lewis Creek National Recreation Trail stretches for 3.7 miles in the Sierra National Forest parallel to Lewis Creek. The trail follows a section of the old Madera Sugar Pine Lumber Company's flume route. From 1900 to 1931, the wooden flume carried lumber 54 miles downstream from the mill

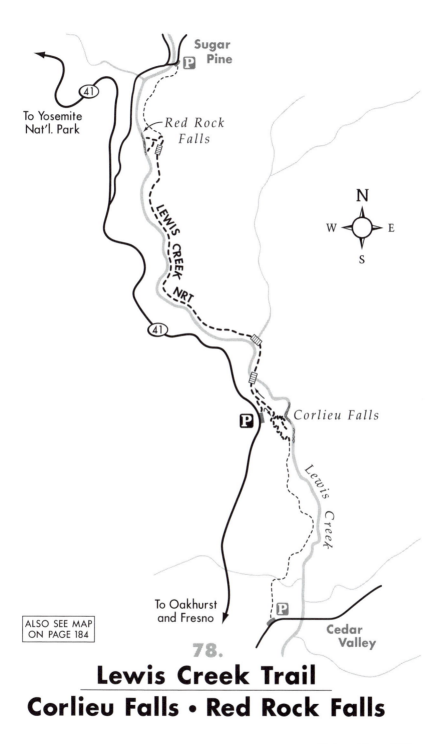

Sugar
Pine
🅿

To Yosemite
Nat'l. Park

Red Rock
Falls

LEWIS CREEK NRT

41

N
W — E
S

🅿

Corlieu Falls

Lewis Creek

🅿

To Oakhurst
and Fresno

Cedar
Valley

ALSO SEE MAP
ON PAGE 184

78.

Lewis Creek Trail
Corlieu Falls • Red Rock Falls

to the town of Madera in the San Joaquin Valley. The historical trail lies between Yosemite and Oakhurst. It connects the communities of Cedar Valley with Sugar Pine along the east side of Highway 41. There are trailheads at each end and one near the middle.

This popular hike takes in the center section of the scenic trail through a forest of ponderosa pine, white fir, oak, and incense cedar. Highlights are Red Rock Falls and Corlieu Falls. Red Rock Falls drops over a wide ledge of red-hued slick rock into a pool surrounded by flat sitting rocks. Corlieu Falls, the highest cataract in Madera County, drops 80 feet over a mossy, fern-covered granite wall in a multi-faceted cascade. The braids of splashing whitewater tumble over rocky shelves and crevices, fanning out into a rock-lined pool.

Driving directions: From the south park entrance, drive 8.6 miles south on Highway 41 to the posted Lewis Creek Trail and parking area on the left.

From Oakhurst, drive 7 miles north on Highway 41 to the posted Lewis Creek Trail and parking area on the right.

Hiking directions: From the north end of the parking area, take the dirt road and descend past the gate into the forest. The road ends at a T-junction with the Lewis Creek Trail. Begin to the right and head downstream toward Corlieu Falls. Pass numerous overlooks of the creek, cascading over granite boulders in the narrow canyon. Zigzag down the canyon, passing more overlooks of Corlieu Falls. At 0.3 miles, a side path veers off to the left. The Lewis Creek Trail continues 1.5 miles on the west canyon wall to Cedar Valley. Instead, bear left and steeply descend to the base of the 80-foot waterfall. Just below the main falls, the path leads 20 yards to the brink of the lower falls, cascading down rock slabs into pools.

Return to the Lewis Creek Trail and head back upstream, passing the trail junction to the parking lot. Cross the log bridge over the creek, and continue up the east side of the cascading whitewater. Wind through a forest of black oak, fir, spruce, and pine, with a lush understory of ferns and wild azaleas. Cross a footbridge over a feeder stream, and pass rock and concrete remnants of an old home. Climb up the east canyon wall, and cross an old wooden bridge to a posted junction. The main trail continues another 0.8 miles to the community of Sugar Pine. Bear left and drop down the hillside to the top of Red Rock Falls and pools. The path to the left leads to the base of the falls and a large but shallow pool. Return along the same route.

79. Willow Creek Trail to Angel Falls and Devil's Slide

Hiking distance: 4.6 miles round trip
Hiking time: 2.5 hours
Elevation gain: 500 feet
Maps: U.S.G.S. Bass Lake

map
page 199

Summary of hike: The North Fork of Willow Creek is a major inlet stream of four-mile-long Bass Lake. The creek forms at Kramer Meadow on the west slope of Fresno Dome and flows south into the upper north end of Bass Lake in the Sierra National Forest. Along the fast-moving creek are Angel Falls and Devil's Slide. Angel Falls plunges over granite rock, forming swirling pools and slickrock slides. (This popular area can be crowded on warm summer days.) Devil's Slide is a long whitewater chute on a polished granite spillway with a final 50-foot drop into a huge, deep pool.

The Willow Creek Trail begins just above the mouth of the creek and moderately climbs to Angel Falls, Devil's Slide, and McLeod Flat. This hike follows the North Fork Willow Creek to both waterfalls, passing a continuous series of dramatic cascades, deep pools, and panoramic vistas.

CAUTION: Near the waterfalls, the rocks are slippery, dangerous, and deadly. Stay on the trail—use common sense and caution.

Driving directions: From the south park entrance, drive 12.6 miles south on Highway 41 to the Bass Lake Road/Road 222 turnoff and turn left. Proceed 3.5 miles east to a road fork. Take the left fork—Road 274—for 0.9 miles to a dirt road on the left, 100 yards before the bridge crossing Willow Creek. Turn left and quickly turn right on the narrow dirt road. Descend 100 yards to the trailhead parking area on the banks of Willow Creek.

From Oakhurst, drive 3 miles north on Highway 41 to the Bass Lake Road/Road 222 turnoff and turn right. Continue with the directions above.

Hiking directions: Walk back to paved Road 274, and cross the bridge on the left over Willow Creek. Bear left on the dirt road, and follow the east side of Willow Creek, overlooking cascades, water chutes, and pools. The road ends in 100 yards by a green structure. Just before reaching the building, cross the wooden footbridge over a side stream to the Willow Creek Trail. Follow the creek upstream through ponderosa pine, California oak, and cedar. Climb to a perch on the east canyon wall. Traverse the hillside to an overlook of Angel Falls, Bass Lake, and the creekside pools. Return to the creek at the brink of the falls by enormous granite slabs, a grouping of jacuzzi-like pools, and slickrock cascades.

The trail continues beyond the falls, staying on the same side of the creek. Pass endless cascades, stair-step waterfalls, and bowl-shaped pools carved into the rock. Side paths descend to the creek. The terrain flattens out and meanders through the forest, passing a large pond formed by the naturally dammed creek. Ascend the canyon again, with glimpses of Devil's Slide through the trees. Side paths descend to pools at the base of the cascade. The forested path continues to climb, emerging along the edge of the massive cascade. Due to past casualties, a fence eliminates access to the smooth, slickrock slide. Beyond Devil's Slide are additional pools and smaller slides.

To hike farther, the trail continues 0.3 miles to a fork. The Chilkoot Trail curves right and heads east to McLeod Flat Road. The Willow Creek Trail continues north, paralleling the creek into McLeod Flat.

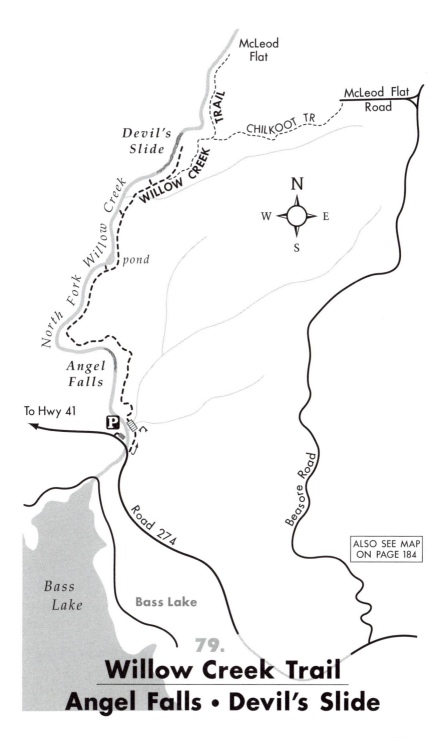

McLeod
Flat

McLeod Flat
Road

*Devil's
Slide*

CHILKOOT TR

WILLOW CREEK TRAIL

North Fork Willow Creek

pond

N

W   E

S

*Angel
Falls*

To Hwy 41

P

Beasore Road

Road 274

ALSO SEE MAP
ON PAGE 184

*Bass
Lake*

Bass Lake

79.

Willow Creek Trail
Angel Falls • Devil's Slide

80. Way-of-the-Mono Interpretive Trail
BASS LAKE

Hiking distance: 0.6-mile loop
Hiking time: 30 minutes
Elevation gain: 200 feet
Maps: U.S.G.S. Bass Lake

Summary of hike: The Mono (Monache) Indians were a hunting and gathering society who lived in the area from the southern Sierras to the coast. The drowned meadow of Crane Valley, where manmade Bass Lake now resides, was home to Mono Indian families, the first inhabitants of the area. The Way-of-the-Mono Interpretive Trail loops around a hillside on the west side of Bass Lake in the Sierra National Forest. The path meanders through a variety of vegetation and crosses a seasonal creek to a spectacular granite rock overlook of Bass Lake and Crane Valley. Atop the overlook are grinding holes left by the valley's previous occupants. The depressions were formed from the preparation of acorn meal. Stations along the trail explain who the Mono Indians were and how they hunted, gathered, and lived in harmony with the land. It is told through the eyes of a 10-year-old Mono Indian girl.

Driving directions: From the south park entrance, drive 12.6 miles south on Highway 41 to the Bass Lake Road/Road 222 turnoff and turn left. Proceed 3.5 miles east to a road fork. Stay on Road 222 to the right. Continue 1.4 miles, staying to the right at a road fork, to the posted nature trail and parking area on the right. The trailhead is located across the road from the signed Little Denver Church Day Use Area.

From Oakhurst, drive 3 miles north on Highway 41 to the Bass Lake Road/Road 222 turnoff and turn right. Continue with the directions above.

Hiking directions: Begin from the right (north) side of the parking area, hiking counter-clockwise. Zigzag up the hillside, passing interpretive panels describing the trees and how the Mono Indians utilized their resources. At the summit, cross a huge granite slab with grinding holes formed from the preparation of acorn meal. From atop the rock are fantastic vistas of Bass Lake and the Crane Valley. After savoring the views, cross the rock slab and pick up the footpath. Wind back down the hillside, returning to the south end of the parking area.

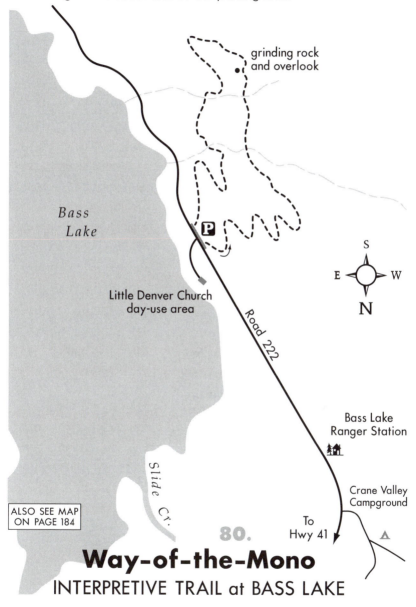

grinding rock
and overlook

Bass
Lake

P

S

E ⊕ W

N

Little Denver Church
day-use area

Road 222

Bass Lake
Ranger Station

Slide Cr.

Crane Valley
Campground

ALSO SEE MAP
ON PAGE 184

80.

To
Hwy 41

Way-of-the-Mono
INTERPRETIVE TRAIL at BASS LAKE

DAY HIKE BOOKS

These books may be purchased at your local bookstore or outdoor shop. Or, order them direct from the distributor:

The Globe Pequot Press

246 Goose Lane • P.O. Box 480 • Guilford, CT 06437-0480
on the web: www.globe-pequot.com

800-243-0495 DIRECT   **800-820-2329** FAX

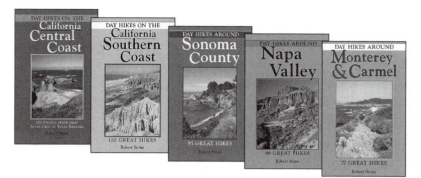

Day Hikes In Sequoia and Kings Canyon National Parks

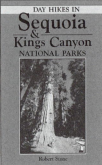

Sequoia and Kings Canyon National Parks must be experienced on foot — only then does one come face-to-face with the scale and grandeur of the incredible scenery. These 61 hikes will introduce you to the world's largest living trees and some of the most impressive canyons, rock formations, and panoramic overlooks found anywhere. Located 30 miles south of Yosemite.

144 pages • 61 hikes • 2001 • 978-1-57342-030-3

Day Hikes Around Sonoma County

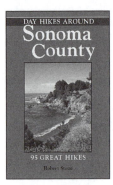

Sonoma County is known for its wineries and a magnificent natural landscape — a picturesque mix of rugged coastline, steep cliffs, forested hillsides, and verdant agricultural valleys. The cities, towns, and villages are as diverse as the geography. Interspersed throughout the landscape are thousands of acres of undeveloped parklands, forests, and open spaces. This collection of 95 of the county's best day hikes provides access to both well-known and out-of-the-way trails.

272 pages • 95 hikes • 2007 • 978-1-57342-053-2

Day Hikes Around Napa Valley

Napa Valley is recognized as one of the premier wine growing regions in the world and a prime tourist destination 50 miles from San Francisco. The broad valley spreads alongside the lush Napa River oasis between two mountain ranges. Agricultural lands blend smoothly with a myriad of regional and state parks and thousands of acres of public greenspace. A wide range of hikes accommodates amateur to avid hikers, from urban strolls to panoramic peak trails.

288 pages • 88 hikes • 2008 • 978-1-57342-057-0

INDEX

About the Author

Since 1991, Robert Stone has been writer, photographer, and publisher of *Day Hike Books*. He is a Los Angeles Times Best Selling Author and an award-winning journalist of Rocky Mountain Outdoor Writers and Photographers, the Outdoor Writers Association of California, and the Northwest Outdoor Writers Association.

Robert has hiked every trail in the *Day Hike Book* series. With 23 hiking guides in the series, many in their third and fourth editions, he has hiked thousands of miles of trails throughout the western United States and Hawaii. When Robert is not hiking, he researches, writes, and maps the hikes before returning to the trails. He spends summers in the Rocky Mountains of Montana and winters on the California Central Coast.